# out of context

**8 Bible Passages
Most Christians Get Wrong**

**Mike Novotny and Bruce Becker**

Published by Straight Talk Books
P.O. Box 301, Milwaukee, WI 53201
800.661.3311 • timeofgrace.org

Copyright © 2020 Time of Grace Ministry

All rights reserved. This publication may not be copied, photocopied, reproduced, translated, or converted to any electronic or machine-readable form in whole or in part, except for brief quotations, without prior written approval from Time of Grace Ministry.

Scripture is taken from THE HOLY BIBLE, NEW INTERNATIONAL VERSION®, NIV®. Copyright © 1973, 1978, 1984, 2011 by Biblica, Inc.® Used by permission. All rights reserved worldwide.

Printed in the United States of America
ISBN: 978-1-949488-40-1

Time of Grace *and* It All Starts Now *are registered marks of Time of Grace Ministry.*

# Contents

Introduction .................................................................................. 4

Context ........................................................................................ 6

"Do Not Judge" ......................................................................... 17

"Where Two or Three Gather in My Name" ........................... 34

"More Than You Can Handle" .................................................. 50

"Plans to Prosper You" ............................................................. 68

What Else Is Out of Context? ................................................... 84

    "Money Is a Root of All Kinds of Evil" ............................... 84

    "I Can Do All Things Through Christ Who Strengthens Me" ..... 93

    "Be Still and Know That I Am God" .................................. 99

    "Forgive and Forget" ........................................................ 104

Conclusion ............................................................................... 122

# Introduction

Do you ever feel a bit lost when it comes to understanding parts of the Bible? You read a verse or a short section of the Bible and you ask yourself, "What does that mean?" Or you see people posting Bible verses in memes on Pinterest and other social media platforms and you wonder if the words are being used the way the Bible authors intended them to be used. Or maybe you hear people using popular sayings that sound like they're from the Bible, but maybe they're not from the Bible at all? How do you know for sure?

One of the key principles to understanding the Bible's meaning of any particular word, verse, section, or book of the Bible is *context*.

In this book, we will take a look at a message series entitled *Out of Context* written and delivered by Pastor Mike Novotny, the lead speaker for Time of Grace. In this series, Pastor Mike describes how four different verses or phrases of the Bible are taken out of context, which changes the meaning of what God originally intended through the inspired authors. These are the sections Pastor Mike addresses:

- "Do not judge"
- "Where two or three gather in my name"
- "More than you can handle"
- "Plans to prosper you"

After each message there are discussion questions to help you dig deeper into the Bible's meaning and give you greater confidence to learn for yourself what the Bible's inspired authors intended you to see and know.

After you go through Pastor Mike's examples, I'll walk you through four additional ones:

- "Money is a root of all kinds of evil"
- "I can do all things through Christ who strengthens me"
- "Be still and know that I am God"
- "Forgive and forget"

Taking these eight statements out of context can lead either to an incomplete or incorrect understanding of God's truth. Understanding them in context gives a richer understanding and appreciation for what God's words say and mean.

*Bruce H. Bucka*

# Context

The dictionary by Merriam-Webster defines the word **con•text** as "the parts of a discourse that surround a word or passage and can throw light on its meaning." Without context, words can mean different things to different people. In context, we can learn the meaning of the words in the Bible as God intended.

Context is like a 1,500-piece puzzle. Examining the individual pieces of the puzzle doesn't tell you much. Sometimes you have no idea how one piece even fits into the puzzle. But when you see the puzzle put together, you have a new perspective that reveals the complete picture.

Let me give you another example. It comes from literature.

In January 1959, an author by the name of Lillian Quigley wrote a children's book entitled, *The Blind Men and the Elephant: An Old Tale From the Land of India*. I remember reading this book when I was in grade school. As the subtitle suggests, this book was based upon a folktale that originated in the ancient Indian subcontinent.

It's the story of a group of six blind men who encountered an elephant for the very first time in their lives. Each of the six men touched a different part of the elephant's body and drew a conclusion about what the elephant was like:

- The first man touched the side of the elephant and concluded that the elephant was like a wall.
- The second man touched the tusk and determined that the elephant was like a spear.
- The third man grabbed the elephant's trunk and stated that the elephant was like a snake.
- The fourth man reached out and put his hands around the elephant's leg and concluded that the elephant was like a tree.

- The fifth man reached up and touched a floppy ear and determined that the elephant was like a fan.
- The sixth man grabbed the elephant's swinging tail and decided the elephant was a like a rope.

Each man drew a conclusion of what the elephant was like based only upon the part of the elephant's body he himself touched. The conclusions of the six men were not wrong, just individually incomplete.

Over the centuries this folktale has been adapted and adopted by different peoples and cultures with each adding their own meaning and significance to the fable. For our purposes, we want to consider a simple reality about the story and apply it to our study of God's Word. Without knowing the larger context of Bible words, verses, sections, and books, we may miss the specific truths that God intends for us.

So where do we go from here?

There are several other important principles that help us understand the context of Bible words, verses, and entire books of the Bible. Let's take a look at these key principles.

## *Origins*

In the Old Testament, there are 39 separate books written over a time frame of about 1,100 years by two dozen or so authors. The New Testament is comprised of 27 separate books written over many decades by nearly a dozen authors. The last book of the Bible was penned more than 1,900 years ago. The significance of this is that there is a multi-century time gap between the authors of the Bible and us, the readers, of the Bible. Just think in terms of your own life, especially if you've had many trips around the yearly calendar. How much different your life is today compared to life in the 1980s or 60s or 40s! Even more so, consider how much different your life is today compared with life 3,500 years ago at the time of Moses, the author of the first five books of the Old Testament.

Each book of the Bible was written by an individual author for another individual or a group of people living at that particular time. Answers to the following questions help us better understand the *who, what, when, where*, and *why* of the book:

- Who was the author?
- What do we know about his personal situation?
- Who was the audience that the author was writing to and what was their personal or social circumstances?
- When and where was it written?
- What was the author's purpose or goal in writing it?

When we read any part of the Bible, *we first need to determine the meaning that the original author intended for the original audience.* Understanding the meaning of the authors original words to an original audience helps remove the distance between the original Bible authors and us as the readers today.

### *Language*

That brings us to a second principle. The original authors of the Bible wrote in one of three languages—Hebrew or Aramaic in the Old Testament and Greek in the New Testament. In reading the Bible, we need to remember that there is a language gap too.

Hebrew is one of a group of languages known as the Semitic languages. These languages were spoken throughout the Middle East, primarily in the region that is the country of Iraq today. The Hebrew language had an alphabet of 22 letters, all consonants. There were no vowels. Imagine trying to play *Scrabble* or *Words With Friends* without any vowels! As time went on, however, the language gurus added vowels to the consonants to make it a more precise language.

The Old Testament was written over the span of 1,000+ years. For the most part, the 39 books were written in the Hebrew language. But there are a few chapters in the books of Ezra and Daniel and one verse in Jeremiah that were written in Aramaic. Aramaic was also a Semitic language and became a popular language in the Middle East. It was the common language spoken in Israel during Jesus' time.

So think about that. Jesus spoke Aramaic during his ministry. Yet when the New Testament authors of Matthew, Mark, Luke, and John—which detail the ministry of Jesus—translated Jesus' words, they translated them into Greek, with a handful of exceptions. There are some Aramaic words that the New Testament authors retained:

- *Raca* meaning "Fool" (Matthew 5:22).
- *Eli, Eli, lema sabachtnani* meaning "My God, My God, why have you forsaken me?" (Matthew 27:46).
- *Talitha koum!* meaning "Little girl, get up!" (Mark 5:41).
- *Ephphatha!* meaning "Be opened!" (Mark 7:34).
- *Hosanna!* meaning "O Lord, save us!" (Mark 11:9).
- *Abba* meaning "Father" (Mark 14:36).
- *Rabboni* meaning "Teacher" (John 20:16).
- *Maranatha* meaning "Lord, come" (1 Corinthians 16:22).

Except for these few Aramaic words, the New Testament was written entirely in the Greek language. So why Greek and not Hebrew or Aramaic?

For a span of hundreds of years before Jesus was born, the Greeks dominated the known world (until around 150 B.C. when the Romans started ruling the world stage), and during that time, Greek became the dominant language.

Around 300 B.C., a translation of the Old Testament from Hebrew to Greek was undertaken. It took a long time to complete, but eventually this translation, known as the Septuagint, became widely used, even among Aramaic-speaking Jews. The bonus of this translation was that non-Semitic peoples, like the Greeks, could now read the Old Testament in their own language.

All of this is to say that Hebrew, Aramaic, and Greek are not familiar languages for most Christians (and non-Christians) in the world today. As the Greeks relied on the Septuagint translation, so we rely on English translations to understand what the original authors wrote and what they meant.

But there are challenges with any translation. It is sometimes difficult to translate the full meaning of a word into a different language. Let me give you an example.

When Jesus was dying on a cross, he spoke (likely in Aramaic) a word that was translated into Greek by the apostle John as *tetelestai*. The English translation of *tetelestai* is, "It is finished." Three English words compared to one Greek word. But that's not even the whole picture. The three English words still don't completely capture the meaning of the one Greek word. *Tetelestai* not only means that Jesus' death on a cross of atoning for the sins of the world was finished or completed but also that the results and benefits of Jesus' death on that cross were permanent, extending into the future. There is a ton packed into that one Greek word.

*So when we read any part of the Bible, we also need to determine the meaning that the original author intended in the original language that he used.*

How do we do that? Bible teachers who have studied the original languages of the Bible can be of great help to us. Commentaries on the various books of the Bible are also helpful. And, personally, you and I can search online to find resources to help us better understand the meaning of words in the original languages of Hebrew, Aramaic, and Greek.

### *Culture*

A third gap that exists is a cultural one. Culture includes people, places, customs, and events. The cultural differences are probably the easiest ones to recognize as we read the Bible. There are many examples of practices and traditions—the way things were done in ancient times—that we can't relate to in our culture.

Here is a list of a few cultural categories. After each category, jot down an example or two of the differences in culture between the people of Bible times and today. You can search your Bible or do some searching online.

Economic:

Geographical:

Transportation:

Agricultural:

Clothing and Shelter:

Political:

Medical:

Educational:

Worship Life:

Music and Entertainment: _____

_____

_____

Marriage and Funeral Practices: _____

_____

_____

*When we read any part of the Bible, we need to understand the culture of the people living at that particular time and place in history.*

## Literary Form

The authors of the books of the Bible used a variety of literary forms to communicate the inspired Word of God. Here is a list of the kinds of literary forms used in the Bible. Keep in mind that some books can be listed in multiple categories.

### Historical Narratives

Historical narratives are factual accounts of what happened at a specific time and place involving specific people and events. A subset of the historical narratives includes the genealogies of God's Old Testament people (Genesis 5, Matthew 1, Luke 3, etc.). Historical books include, among many others, Genesis, Exodus, Joshua, Ruth, Esther, Matthew, Mark, Luke, John, and Acts.

### Laws and Statutes

Much of what is found in the first five books of the Bible is focused on laws, rules, and regulations for God's Old Testament people. The most well-known set of laws is the Ten Commandments. Genesis, Exodus, Leviticus, Numbers, and Deuteronomy comprise the primary books of the Bible in this category.

*Hebrew Poetry*
Unlike English poetry, which often has a rhythmic aspect to it, Hebrew poetry is more about the structure of the text, repetition, and meter. The psalms contain a large portion of the Bible's poetry.

*Wisdom Literature*
Wisdom literature includes pithy statements of common rules for life in a general sense. Wisdom literature, however, is not to be understood in a guaranteed, universal sense. Proverbs, Ecclesiastes, and Song of Songs all deal with daily living and human relationships.

*Prophecy*
The prophets were the mouthpieces of God. They spoke God's Word to God's people. They would proclaim what God instructed them to proclaim. Sometimes the proclamation had current relevance. Other times it had future relevance. When it came to future relevance, there were prophecies in which there was a near-term fulfillment as well as a long-term fulfillment. The last half of the Old Testament is where the majority of prophecy is recorded. A subset of this literary form are the visions that contain prophetic, symbolic language, often quite intense symbolism. Such visions occur in Ezekiel, Daniel, and Revelation.

*Parables*
Jesus often used parables. They were a unique way of communicating stories that had a single point of emphasis. Sometimes

Jesus taught a parable so that his followers would understand his point and his enemies wouldn't, because the point of the parable required faith to understand it. There are dozens of Jesus' parables recorded in Matthew, Mark, Luke, and John. There are also a couple of examples in the Old Testament—Judges chapter 9 and 2 Samuel chapter 12.

*Epistle/Letter*
Epistles were personal correspondences that were written to either a particular individual or a group of people, i.e., a congregation. The letters often contained teaching, encouragement, and warnings on tough issues facing the church. The epistles comprise most of the New Testament, beginning with Romans and ending with Jude.

Understanding the literary form that the author used helps us do the following:

- Recognize that *historical narratives* are facts that actually happened.
- Understand that *laws and statutes* were given for a particular group of people at a particular time.
- Appreciate the structured text and repetition in *Hebrew poetry* and the meaning contained in it.
- Avoid concluding that *wisdom literature* speaks universal truths rather than general rules for life.
- Recognize *prophecy* as God's words spoken through the prophets.
- Avoid reading too much into each *parable* and focus on the one main point.
- Understand that these were *letters* to real people with real problems but ones that we can apply to our own lives.

*When we read any part of the Bible, we need to understand the literary form that the author uses so that we treat the words as the author intended.*

Let's now look at Pastor Mike Novotny's *Out of Context* message series to help us better understand reading the Bible in context.

# "Do Not Judge"

*Matthew 7:1-6*

Have you ever felt like you just had to say something? When you witness someone doing something that you know is dangerous—going down a dark, difficult, and sinful path—but you know to say something would be complicated and hard and difficult? The person will probably be defensive, but something within you just isn't okay with staying silent. When you and I see people whom we love doing something that God doesn't like, so often our Christian consciences are burdened with a desire and a compulsion to say something.

Just before we get up the courage to say something, there are these three words from the Bible that often float into our heads, the words that some people think are the most quoted words from Scripture in contemporary culture. These words come from Matthew 7:1: **"Do not judge."** That seems pretty clear, right? Do you know who said those words? Jesus. He said, "Don't judge." Who are you and I as imperfect, broken, sinful people to look down and correct the behavior of other imperfect, broken, sinful people?

Do you know what *judging* means if you'd look up that word? "To say that something is good or bad." That means you're a judgmental person if you say that anything is good or bad. If you see someone being kind and generous with a little kid and you say, "That's great," you're being judgmental. When someone tweets something that's really sexist or racist and you say, "That's not right," you are being judgmental. If you think that bosses and religious leaders shouldn't abuse the people at their companies or in their churches, you are being judgmental. When you think that feeding the poor and stopping sex trafficking are good things for our planet, you're being judgmental. The guy who marches around a military funeral with a sign in his hand with something vile about

God is being judgmental. And if you think it's vile, you are being judgmental too.

In fact, this is so important that I'd love for you to highlight it here: *All people, including you, including me, spend all day being judgmental.* If you don't like that sentence, you are being judgmental. If Jesus said, "Do not judge," you know that Christians shouldn't be judgmental. But something doesn't seem right because when Jesus said, "Don't be like that," his words in and of themselves were a form of being judgmental. Every value judgment and every categorizing of something as good or bad is being judgmental. All people, religious or not, fundamentalist Christians or atheists, spend all day long being judgmental. Jesus had standards; he didn't want people to throw out the whole idea of right or wrong. So what exactly did he mean when he said, "Do not judge"?

Don't some of the biggest problems that we read in the headlines of America today happen because people weren't judgmental enough? The Hollywood director was a pervert, and people on the set knew it. But no one stepped forward to say anything or judge it as bad. No one raised the standard of behavior. And because people weren't judgmental, some poor actress walked into his office for the first time and got hurt. A pastor, a priest, or a business leader takes advantage of his or her position; people get hurt. She takes money; he abuses people sexually. What happens if people who know about it don't say, "We can't stand for this. We need a higher standard of behavior"? If no one's judgmental, then what happens?

When you don't call bad things bad, when you don't call sinful things sinful, people get hurt because that's what bad things do; they hurt people. Some people would say that religious people are way too judgmental; they have to stop. While other people would say many of us are not being judgmental enough; we need more of it. So what exactly should we do? And when it's not some Hollywood headline but it's happening in your family or in your workplace or in your church or in your circle of friends, when you see something bad or wrong and you don't want to be like that hypocritical person, you just want to stop bad things from hurting people, what do you say?

What exactly did Jesus mean with those famous words "Do not judge"? I have some really good news. Jesus' answer to that question is crystal clear. If you would read the context, what he meant when he said those words is so simple to understand. I want to teach you not just about that quote but the context too. I want to dig in not only to Matthew 7:1, but I want us to look at the whole paragraph of what Jesus taught. That way the next time you see someone you love doing something that God himself does not love, you'll know exactly what to say and how to say it.

Let's jump into Jesus' words in Matthew chapter 7; he started like this in verses 1 and 2: **"Do not judge, or you too will be judged. For in the same way you judge others, you will be judged, and with the measure you use, it will be measured to you."** That helps already, doesn't it? When you think about interpreting the Bible or understanding Jesus correctly, you should circle little transition words like the word "for" in the second line. *For* is essentially Jesus' chance to explain himself. He said, "You shouldn't judge." You can interpret that in a whole bunch of ways. *For* is his way of saying exactly what he meant, and you can see what Jesus meant. He was saying, "In the same way you judge those people, those people are going to judge you." The same standard of behavior that you want people to measure up to is the same standard they're going to use when they turn around and measure you.

Let's think of it like a tape measure. The Bible says that Christians, when it comes to sexuality or sobriety, have a standard we should measure up to—say 2 feet on the tape measure. I might be absolutely right about that as I read the Bible, but I have to know that as soon as I open my mouth and judge someone by this standard, this is going to happen: They're going to take the tape measure and set it next to me. If I'm going to talk about your sex life, your work ethic, your drinking habits, or how you are in relationships, I have to know that instinctively you're going to borrow my tape measure and see if I measure up.

Jesus said that what you can't do is you can't say, "Here's God's standard," and then when it comes to yourself, have a different standard. You can't say, "The Bible says . . ." but then have a different lifestyle that doesn't measure up to what the Bible says. Jesus said that if that's what you're going to do, then don't judge, or you're going to be judged. Every person has a little inner defense lawyer who loves to borrow the tape measure. Before you open your mouth—and you might have to—make sure you know that judgment is coming right back to you. In fact, Jesus said this is important because if you change the standard of measurement, you won't just lose the chance to correct bad behavior; the conversation will blow up and hurt people in an even worse way.

That's what Jesus went on to say in the next verses; check out verses 3 and 4: **"Why do you look at the speck of sawdust in your brother's eye and pay no attention to the plank in your own eye? How can you say to your brother, 'Let me take the speck out of your eye,' when all the time there is a plank in your own eye?"**

He said, "How is it possible that you would look at something so small, like a speck of sawdust or a little sliver, and pay no attention to the two-by-four that's literally sticking out of your own face?" Jesus was exaggerating; he was cracking a joke to say how ridiculous it is to be so concerned about someone's little thing and so unconcerned about your own big thing. Sometimes you can see in your neighbor, your brother, your friend, your boss something that's not right, something that's dangerous. Everything in you can get so focused on that little sliver that you want to take it out. But Jesus said, "How can you take that out if there's a plank sticking out of your face?"

Notice the language that Jesus used. He said, "Why do you look at this speck and pay no attention to your plank? Why are you so infatuated with behavior, with correcting, with seeing the danger and the problem with this little thing, but it's as if you have no concern, no desire, to change yourself? You don't even pay attention to your big thing."

It kind of reminds me of a famous commercial from 1987 from the American Anti-Drug Council; maybe you remember it. This dad barges into his teenage son's bedroom holding a box full of drug paraphernalia. The dad says to the kid, "Are these your drugs? Where did you get it? Who taught you how to do this stuff?" And the son's response? "You, alright! I learned it from you, Dad." Then the voiceover comes on: "Parents who use drugs have children who use drugs," and the commercial ends. It's like the father saw this speck, this dangerous thing: "My kid's getting high. We've got to deal with this." But he missed something major in his own life. Jesus said be very, very careful. If you're going to follow him, if you're going to be his disciple, if you're going to take sin seriously—and you should—be careful that you don't look at slivers in others and pay no attention to the plank in yourself.

I once heard a pastor say that very often the speck and the plank are made out of the same wood. Sometimes the thing that drives you crazy about your daughter is kind of the same thing that you do. Sometimes the same sin that seems so obvious in others is a sin you often commit yourself.

Have you ever been at a park and seen a dad turn to his kids and yell, "Stop yelling!"? Have you ever seen a husband and a wife in an argument, and he says, "You always try to win," as he tries to win with that exaggeration? If you're the proud person in the room and someone else comes in with a lot of pride, you'll notice it instantly and hate it. If you're sinfully overcompetitive and you always have to win and a version of you walks into the room or onto the field, you're going to notice that person and despise him or her. It's the vain woman who cares way too much about the way she looks who notices the vanity in another woman at her job. It's the person who has to get the last word in an argument who goes crazy when someone else at work has to get the last word in an argument. The speck and the plank are very often the same thing, and it's so clear. We see it, we look at it in other people, but we pay no attention to it in ourselves.

So Jesus asked the question, "Well, why?" Did you notice that in verse 3? Why do you look at that speck but pay no attention to the plank? There are some really good answers to that question. Why do we notice the sin in other people? Why are Christians, religious people in particular, so quick to judge? We know that other people's sin is dangerous. A little sliver, a speck, might seem small compared to a plank, but if a little speck was literally in someone's eye, it would be dangerous. If a piece of a contact, if a little bug, if an eyelash in your eye can do damage and drive you crazy, then even a speck isn't to be taken lightly. And so often it's the most biblically minded people, those who are the most passionate about their religion and faith, who see that when other people don't.

I get why the world thinks that Christians are often judgmental because sometimes it's only the people who are closest to Christ who realize how bad run-of-the-mill, everyday sins really are. Where many people might excuse it and say, "Well, no one's perfect, and everybody sins. We're all broken; we're all messed up. God is love; we're all going to be fine." But it's the Christian who's read Jesus' teaching who knows that if you do this and if you don't take this out of your soul, it will cause major damage to you, to other people, and even to your eternity.

The apostle Paul's words in 1 Corinthians 6:9,10 explain this: **"Don't be deceived: Neither the sexually immoral nor idolaters nor adulterers nor men who have sex with men nor thieves nor the greedy nor drunkards nor slanderers nor swindlers will inherit the kingdom of God."** It explains why we look at the speck but don't always see the plank.

If our knowledge of the Bible makes us take this more seriously than most people, how could it be possible that the most religious people would miss the planks? Here's the best answer that I have: We think our sin is different. Sometimes the speck and the plank are made out of the same kind of wood, but sometimes they're not. And sometimes his behavior or her behavior or our friend's behavior is just so confusing to us that it seems like we have to say something.

This happens a ton generationally. Sometimes the sins we struggle with stereotypically as older people or younger people or from this generational culture or this one are so different that we spend our time focused on how a different generation can be doing what they do.

Maybe you've heard the stereotypes. Older Christians look at millennials and talk about their work ethic. "How many times are you going to change majors and change jobs. If something gets hard, are you just going to bail? You have no commitment. You won't join a church; you won't join anything because you have no perseverance or endurance." It's so easy to look at a different generation and see its flaws and point a finger.

What do millennials do right back? They look at their parents, their grandparents, and they think, "Yeah, like I'd want to have a faith like yours?" "Mom and Dad, you always post that stuff on Facebook about immigrants—do you know that Jesus was an immigrant? that he fled to Egypt? that when God's people came out of the Promise Land, they were immigrants?" "You snap judgments about what people should do and about political issues." "You didn't get divorced because you were religious, but I would never want to have a relationship like yours." "Dad, you said you were providing for us while you were never home, and I'm not going to do that to my kids." And one Christian looks at another Christian, and the sins seem so different. We notice those sins in an instant, but we can't see something in ourselves.

Here's the thing though, our sins might seem different on paper, but do you know the root problem, the common denominator? We all love to think about sins that we don't commit, and we love to ignore the ones that we do. We all love to quote the passages that we're doing pretty well with and want to skip by the pages that convict us and ask us to change. We come to church with selective listening. We latch on to some passages and ignore others, and people get hurt.

Think about Jesus' speck/plank analogy. Let's say you have a speck in your eye, but I don't deal with my own sin. If there's a plank actually sticking out of my face and I try to get close to get your speck, do you know what will happen? I'll smack you in the face before I even get to the speck. Every time I try to talk about your speck, I would do more damage because my hypocrisy is so evident to you that you'll never have the hard conversation about your speck until I deal with my plank. And that's exactly why Jesus said that before we deal with others' sin, we've got to start with our own.

Look what he said in Matthew 7:5: **"You hypocrite, first take the plank out of your own eye, and then you will see clearly to remove the speck from your brother's eye."** I love that. When someone claims that the Bible says, "Do not be judgmental," immediately open your Bible and quote this verse, because this is what Jesus actually meant. He said, "Are you concerned about removing that speck from your brother's eye? Do you think that behavior's wrong and sinful and dangerous and needs to be dealt with? The answer is, God does too! Do you think that person needs to repent and change and get help? The answer is yes; God agrees with you. Are you right about the passage that you quote and measuring behavior? You're probably right; the Bible does say that, but before you have that conversation, you have to have a different conversation."

Let me highlight here what Jesus was saying. He was saying:

First, deal with you, and then you can deal with them. First, you've got to look at the man in the mirror. First, you've got to ask him to make a change (to quote Michael Jackson). And then, you can actually have the conversation about another person's sin without it blowing up in hypocrisy.

If you don't do that, Jesus knows exactly what's going to happen. Let me show you the toughest verse in this section, verse 6: **"Do not give dogs what is sacred; do not throw your pearls to pigs. If you do, they may trample them under their feet, and turn and tear you to pieces."**

That's a really difficult verse to interpret. The sacred thing, the pearls that Jesus was talking about, is the Bible. Now I'm about to have a conversation with you about your behavior, and I'm going to open the Bible and share the sacred Word of God. This is a precious pearl that Jesus has given to us, but if I do it as a hypocrite, if I have a plank in my face and I'm bringing the Bible, you know what's going to happen? You're going to trample it under your feet. You're not going to listen to me or respect the Bible or be so grateful that I quoted that passage. Instead, you're going to trample the Word, despise when someone quotes it to you, and then you're going to turn and tear me to pieces. The sacred Word of God will be damaged; our relationship will be damaged because I didn't start with myself. Instead, I just wanted to talk about you. But if I deal with myself first, if I come to you humbly, if I admit my sin, if I'm not coming as a hypocrite but as a fellow sinner who relies on the grace of God, then maybe, just maybe, we can talk about you.

Put it all together in context and what exactly was Jesus teaching? In context, Jesus said, "Do not judge . . . yet." There's a time when you need to judge; you're going to have to talk about bad behavior and correct sins. But before you have that conversation, just wait. You can judge, but just not yet.

Let's answer one final question: *How?* If we're going to start with ourselves, if we're going to deal with our planks, how can we do that? If it's so easy to be blind to our own sins, how can we learn to see them? Let me give you three quick answers to that question.

1. Grow by reading the Bible. Read paragraphs and chapters and books, and God's going to deal with your plank.
2. Unless your health impedes you, gather with a church family.
3. Gather with other Christians so you can ask one of the most dangerous and helpful questions of all: What don't I see?

If you do those three things, it won't make the conversation easy, but it will make it better. Because if you deal with your own sins and your own plank, do you know what's going to happen? You're going to be really, really thankful for Jesus.

Every time I speak in church or write about a certain section of Scripture, I look at the section for the good news. Where's the hope? People don't just pick up books or come to church to get Bible-slapped. So where's the grace and the forgiveness and the compassion in Matthew 7:1-6? To be honest, I read these verses a dozen times, and it's not there. There's no warm, fuzzy ending. But then I thought, "Why did Jesus say it?" He said it because he didn't want his followers to be self-righteous and proud. He wanted them to be able to see their own sin and follow him to a cross.

If you do the same thing, if the Holy Spirit and a good Christian community help you see that your sin is substantial yet there is a God who took care of all of it, it helps you see that you need Jesus. Jesus didn't have a splinter, a speck, or a plank. He had a cross made of wood, and he died on it for the forgiveness of all of our pride and judgmentalism and sin. When you kneel every morning at the foot of the cross and say, "God, you had mercy on me. When I was ignorant, when I was too zealous, when I was too proud, you were so patient with me, so loving." And if every day you can start as a humble sinner who's been forgiven by the love of God, you'll be ready to have a hard conversation.

# Questions for Personal Reflection and/or Group Discussion

Pastor Mike said:

*What exactly did Jesus mean with those famous words "Do not judge"? I have some really good news. Jesus' answer to that question is crystal clear. If you would read the context, what he meant when he said those words is so simple to understand.*

If the words "do not judge" are crystal clear and so simple to understand, why do so many people not understand them as Jesus taught them?

Christians are sometimes reluctant to judge others. What do you think are the reasons for that reluctance?

Pastor Mike said:

*When you think about interpreting the Bible or understanding Jesus correctly, you should circle little transition words like the word "for" in the second line.* For *is essentially Jesus' chance to explain himself. He said, "You shouldn't judge." You can interpret that in a whole bunch of ways.* For *is his way of saying exactly what he meant, and you can see what Jesus meant.*

Using a Bible concordance or an online Bible search tool, find other examples of transition words like *for* or *so* or *therefore*. Identify the truth that the *for*, *so*, or *therefore* is referring to.

Pastor Mike said:

*He said, "How is it possible that you would look at something so small, like a speck of sawdust or a little sliver, and pay no attention to the two-by-four that's literally sticking out of your own face?" Jesus was exaggerating; he was cracking a joke to say how ridiculous it is to be so concerned about someone's little thing and so unconcerned about your own big thing.*

What are some reasons for why we, as individuals, have trouble seeing the planks in our own eyes?

Pastor Mike said:

*I once heard a pastor say that very often the speck and the plank are made out of the same wood.*

Evaluate this statement about the speck and plank being made out of the same wood.

Are you able to identify any specks you see in others that you also struggle with big time in your own life?

Pastor Mike said:

*Put it all together in context and what exactly was Jesus teaching? In context, Jesus said, "Do not judge . . . yet." There's a time when you need to judge; you're going to have to talk about bad behavior and correct sins. But before you have that conversation, just wait. You can judge, but just not yet.*

What did Pastor Mike mean when he said that we can judge others, but just not yet?

_____

_____

_____

_____

_____

What are some examples of how the words "do not judge" have been taken out of context?

_____

_____

_____

_____

_____

Pastor Mike said:

*How? If we're going to start with ourselves, if we're going to deal with our planks, how can we do that? If it's so easy to be blind to our own sins, how can we learn to see them? Let me give you three quick answers to that question.*

What were the three answers that Pastor Mike suggested?

Do you have any additional answers to how we deal with the planks in our own eyes?

# "Where Two or Three Gather in My Name"

*Matthew 18:15-20*

*(When you read the title of this section, "Where Two or Three Gather in My Name," what comes to mind? Has anyone ever suggested to you that it refers to worship? Although Jesus is present when Christians gather to worship, worship is not the context of this phrase. Pastor Mike will explain . . .)*

A few weeks ago I was in the basement of a guy who used to be a pastor, rummaging through box after box of the books that he used when he was in ministry. As we went through all those boxes, he started to tell me the story of why being a pastor was part of his past and no longer part of his present. It was complicated, like all situations like that are, but he told me it's because he wanted to practice at his church this one thing that Jesus preached in Matthew chapter 18. When he came forward to his church and said he planned on practicing it, the church said, "You can't and you won't and if you try, you can't be our pastor anymore."

After a lot of nights of agonizing prayer with his wife, his friends, and with people whom he trusted, he stepped away from the church and left the ministry. As we went through all those boxes, he came across a book that was actually about the topic that Jesus covered in Matthew chapter 18, and he said, "Mike, did you know that at our church we actually read this book as a church leadership team? When we read it, people said they loved it; this was the right thing to do that Jesus taught. But when it came time to actually practice it, everything changed."

Now before you judge that church, I should tell you something. My church—in its about decade-long history—has never fully practiced what Jesus preached in Matthew chapter 18. In my career as a pastor, over 13 years now, I have never fully followed every step that Jesus taught in that chapter either. In fact, when I reached out to the secretary of our parent campus, which has existed for 150 years, I told her, "Find me the last time this happened at our church." She looked back decades and decades and couldn't find a single time. She jokingly said, "Do you want me to check when the church council minutes were written in German?" Because she couldn't find anything in English.

Do you know what Jesus taught in Matthew chapter 18? A teaching that was so hard that a church would rather get a new pastor than practice it? Here's a snippet of how Jesus started in verse 15: **"If your brother or sister sins."** Jesus was talking about sin that happens in the church among Christian people. He wasn't addressing the kind of sins that happen with our friends and our family members and our neighbors who don't believe in Jesus. This is about what happens when sin happens in the church.

The truth is that most of the time that teaching isn't that difficult because when a Christian sins—thought something or did something or said something that wasn't in line with Jesus—they recognize it and don't want to do it anymore. They repent and apologize. And as brothers and sisters in the church, we get to do the easiest and most beautiful thing; we get to tell people about Jesus. We get to remind them that there's forgiveness and mercy for sin and Jesus died for it at the cross.

But what happens when a brother or a sister doesn't want to stop that sin? What happens when they sin, but they don't really seem that sorry for it? What happens when they hold on to the sin and plan on doing it over and over again? What if they're not ashamed but proud of it? What does a Christian do then?

When your best friend is flirting with a married man or your best friend is about to abandon his wife and kids because he thinks he's found something better, what do you do? When she says she doesn't have time to serve her family, but she has time to stare at her phone. When he claims he doesn't have money to help the poor, but he gets the latest upgrade and is paying $200+ a month for cable. What do you do? When someone claims to be a follower of Jesus, what do you do when instead of struggling with the sin and battling it, it's repetitive and a pattern and that person doesn't seem all that broken up about it?

If you read the previous section of this book, you know exactly what to do. Jesus said when you see a sin in another Christian's life, before you speak a syllable to them about their sin, you need to think about your own sin. Jesus said, "Judge not, or you will be judged." Make sure the standard you're holding other Christians to is the standard you're holding yourself to. Don't measure their behavior with money or marriage or sexuality or whatever before you measure yourself.

But let's assume you've done that. Let's assume you're not a pretender, not a hypocrite, and you really do care about God's will. You're trying to own your sin, repent of it, and grow, but this brother or sister doesn't seem to. What do you do then? That's what Jesus lays out in Matthew chapter 18. If you didn't get my drift just yet, it's going to be hard. It's so hard that many churches, sometimes whole denominations, don't practice what Jesus preached.

Here are the four stages that Jesus laid out for dealing with sin. Jesus said, "When a brother or sister sins and doesn't seem all that repentant or sorry, the very first thing you and I should do is *to go and to show on the down low*." Here's how Jesus said it: **"If your brother or sister sins, go and point out their fault, just between the two of you. If they listen to you, you have won them over"** (Matthew 18:15). Unless there are extenuating circumstances like someone's in danger, you should keep this conversation as small and quiet and private as possible for as long as possible.

This is where it gets hard, right? Most of us, even as Christians, don't love conflict, even if the conversation is a good one to have.

Most of us get really anxious about these kinds of conversations. We love it when people like us, and people tend not to like us when we have these kinds of conversations. So what we tend to do, even as Jesus' followers, is to talk *about* people instead of talking *to* people. Jesus knows it's tempting to talk about someone: "Are you guys concerned about so and so? I was kind of bothered at the Bible study when she said . . ." Yes, it's hard to talk to someone about a sin, but Jesus knows it's impossible to fix unless we actually talk to that person. So he says, **"If your brother or sister sins, go and point out their fault, just between the two of you."** It just might work.

I love the hope that Jesus gives. He says that if they listen to you, you have won them over. But what if they don't listen? What if after not just one conversation but a dozen conversations and texts and emails, what if they shut you out? What if they say you're being judgmental and this is none of your business and how I live my life is between me and God? What if they won't even return your texts anymore or communicate? What if they bail on you? What do you do then?

Well, that's stage two of Jesus' plan. He said if it gets to that point, then you *go and show but not so low*. Here's how Jesus put it: **"But if they will not listen, take one or two others along, so that 'every matter may be established by the testimony of two or three witnesses'"** (verse 16).

Sometimes, when you go with a witness, do you know what happens? The person listens. Maybe at first they assumed you were a super judgmental person from their congregation, but now that you're with a witness they know, "Wow, maybe this is serious? Maybe I need to think about that. Because I respect those people, and I know that they love me and are concerned for me." And if that person listens to you at that point, do you know what you get to do? You get to give them Jesus!

But what if they don't listen? What if they push you away even more? What if they don't want to listen to two or three people who are gathered around an open Bible? Then Jesus says you move to stage three, and stage three is *to go and let the church know*. Here's how Jesus put it in verse 17: **"If they still refuse to listen, tell it to the church."**

Ideally, this would be the first time when I as a pastor or the pastor at your church would find out about the sin in your circle of friends or your family. You would tell the leadership of your church, and at that point, they would try to do anything possible to save the wandering sinner. Jesus didn't tell us the exact way to do this, but I could imagine that I would gather my members as a church family, we would have a special meeting, and I would have to tell you the name of the person who's caught up in sin and the sin that they're committing. I'd have to open a Bible and show my members why we're so concerned for this person's soul, and I would plead with them: "Do any of you know her? Do any of you have other information about him? Why is she pushing us away? Is there something going on in his past history that would mean we need to be more patient and not move forward too quickly?" And as a church, we would do anything and everything because someone's eternity is at stake. We would go all out communicating our concern.

If that person listens, do you know what you get to give him or her? Jesus.

What if the whole church gets involved? What if the pastor calls and emails and texts and shows up on the person's doorstep and they still push away? They still hold on to their sin? Then we move to the final stage: *we go and we let the unbeliever know*. Here's what Jesus said at the end of verse 17: **"And if they refuse to listen even to the church, treat them as you would a pagan or a tax collector."**

What do you think that means? Didn't Jesus love pagans and unbelieving people? Yes. Didn't he reach his arms out in love and have meals with people like Matthew and his tax-collecting friends? Absolutely. Would we keep on loving this person who's holding on to their sin? Would we reach out to them? Absolutely. But do you know the one thing Jesus didn't do with pagans? He didn't act like they weren't pagans. He didn't treat them as God-fearing, grace-believing people. He didn't act as though they'd be okay if they took their last breath and died that day.

This is the brutally hard step that the church is called to do. If after all those conversations a person who claims to be a Christian is still holding on to their sin, you and I would essentially have to tell them this: "You might say that you love God, but you don't because love for God is to obey his commands. You don't even want to obey his command. You might think that you have a personal relationship with Jesus as your Savior, but, listen, you don't. Jesus said if you would believe in him, you would love the things that he taught, but you love the things that Jesus hated. You might think that you have the Holy Spirit in your heart, but you don't because the Holy Spirit inspired every verse in the Bible and you don't even want to hear the things he wrote in this book." We would have to say with broken hearts and tears in our eyes, "If you were to take your last breath today, if a car accident happened, if you had a stroke in the middle of the night, you would not go to a better place. You would die as a pagan, and you would suffer in hell."

Can I be real with you? The reason I as a pastor have never gotten to that point is because sinners are cowards. Because instead of repenting, instead of trying to give the church the reason that they could still be a Christian and live in sin, they run. They run. If there's one thing as a pastor that breaks my heart, it's when people run and think they're fine. They think they're good with Jesus. They think the church is being judgmental. They think, "Who are these Christians to look at my behavior when they're imperfect themselves?" They run. And they say, "Thanks for everything in the past, but I don't need you to be my pastor anymore. Thanks for everything with the church, but I'm going to find a new church home." Likely they go and find a place and a pastor who has no clue about their sin so they can hold on to it knowing no one knows.

I have no clue what to do at that point. Do I text them every week, even if they never text me back? Do I show up on their doorstep unannounced saying, "I'm not going to let you go!" Do we send a letter signed by the church's leadership team, "Hey! We think you're going to hell." What do you and I do when we need to have the hardest conversation in a person's life? If that person is going to run, what do we say? If we're the family of God, how could we watch someone run away from God? In Jesus' day, a person probably lived in a small village and saw the people from their spiritual community and couldn't run from it, but today people can. And if someone wants to hold on to their sin and live in it, there's a hundred churches that they could go to and a hundred pastors who won't have a clue. No wonder no one practices Matthew chapter 18, right?

Here's Jesus' reason why we should follow his four stages. The simple answer is . . . love. We would give up all of our comfort for the sake of love. Isn't that true? When you really love someone, you get uncomfortable for them. Or to quote Jesus, why would a Good Shepherd leave 99 percent of his flock who are bedded down for the night on the soft grass under the starry sky? Why would he get up and go into wolf-infested, dark valleys? Because of love. Because getting the 99 percent on the Savior sheep test is not good enough for a Good Shepherd. With his reckless love, there is no valley so dark he wouldn't go into it to find a sheep that's lost.

I can make you this guarantee: If you are a member of my church and you hold on to sin, if I'm worried that you wouldn't see Jesus for ever and ever, I will hunt you down. It will be awkward, and you might hate me or despise me. You might regret having given me your contact information because I'm going to blow up your phone, and I'm not going to let you go. Not because I hate you, not because I think I'm better than you, but because I love you. Your eternity matters way too much to me and way too much to Jesus to just watch it happen. Love has to confront a sin. Love can't abide bad behavior because sin hurts people, and God doesn't want to hurt people.

That's why Jesus said this next in really strong terms: **"Truly I tell you, whatever you bind on earth will be bound in heaven, and whatever you loose on earth will be loosed in heaven"** (verse 18). For the church to bind someone's sin on earth is like taking a roll of church duct tape and wrapping this sin in a person's hands and telling them, "This is stuck to you. You're going to come to church and listen to Christian radio and people are going to talk about how Jesus takes away sin, but not yours. It's bound to you because you want to hold on to it; you don't want Jesus to take this because it's your sin."

Here's the crazy part of what Jesus said—Whatever you bind on earth will be bound in heaven. We aren't being judgmental church people. If we're doing this according to the Bible, then what Jesus sees in heaven is just what we say on earth. The sin is stuck to that person. However, whatever you loose on earth—if by the grace of God that person says, "Oh! I almost gave up my soul. I almost cashed in my eternity for some relationship? for some sin? for some joy ride? for 5, 10, 50 years?" If they realize that and repent, this is the amazing thing we get to do: we get to give that person Jesus. We get to undo the church duct tape, and we get to take away their sin. We get to welcome them back and say, "You know, that's not just me telling you you're forgiven and loved. That's what Jesus says in heaven; it has been loosed in the presence of God himself."

That's why we do it. We love someone so much that we don't want them to stand before Jesus with the one thing that Jesus can't stand. Which is why we need Jesus' final words. At the end of this section, Jesus said something that pastors love to quote out of context. He said, **"Truly I tell you that if two of you on earth agree about anything they ask for, it will be done for them by my Father in heaven. For where two or three gather in my name, there am I with them"** (verses 19,20). "When you're reaching out to someone you love and they're not changing and you feel like you can't do it, I'm right there," God says.

Here's the big idea I want you to remember when you need to have a hard conversation: *God is here*. When you're trying to find the courage to talk to that person instead of about that person, you can remember that God is here. And when you feel like you have to bring one or two witnesses and you're waiting at the coffee shop and you can just read her body language before you say a word, you can remember that God is here. When the church is having a meeting and it feels so heavy and you just wish you could talk about easier things, you can remember that God is here. When you have to write the hardest letter in your church's history and tell a person you've excommunicated them from the family of God, when your ink is trying to dodge the tears falling from your cheeks, you can remember that God is here. This person might listen to you and they might not, but God is here. This might ruin your friendship, to be honest, but it's worth it for the sake of eternity, and God is here. And someone might post this letter on Facebook and people might assume your church is just one of "those" kind of churches, but God is here.

I want you to remember that. As you and I try to love people in a better way than we ever have before, as we stop embracing the American value of tolerance that lets people walk away from Jesus, remember that God is here.

Last Sunday after church, I was hanging out with some pastors at night around a bonfire. I asked them this question: "Have you guys ever done Matthew 18 in your entire ministries?" It got really quiet. But there was this older pastor who was just about to leave.

He had his lawn chair in his hand and was walking away. He turned around as a memory stirred. He said, "You know, Mike, decades ago we had to tell it to the church. This woman in our congregation was holding on to her sin. She wasn't changing it, and I told the church one day. I didn't tell the name just yet, but I told them we need to have a meeting about someone we're concerned about. And the sister-in-law of the sinner actually ran up to me and she said, 'Are you talking about my sister-in-law?' And I said, 'Yeah, I am.' And she said, 'Can I try to reach out?' He said, 'Of course.' And so she did, and do you know what happened? She listened."

For some reason that one person got through, and the Holy Spirit stirred in the sinner's heart. I was sitting there at the fire and looking at the pastor's face. A smile kind of crept across his expression. He said, "You know what, Mike? I still get the newsletters from that church even though I haven't been there in 20 years. And do you know whose name I see worshiping and serving? Hers."

Does it always work out that well? Not always. Will people always listen when you have a good, biblical conversation about sin? Not always. Will some souls be saved because of your bravery and your love? Sometimes. Will Jesus be with you no matter what happens? Always.

# Questions for Personal Reflection and/or Group Discussion

Pastor Mike said:

*Let's assume you're not a pretender, not a hypocrite, and you really do care about God's will. You're trying to own your sin, repent of it, and grow, but this brother or sister doesn't seem to. What do you do then? That's what Jesus lays out in Matthew chapter 18. If you didn't get my drift just yet, it's going to be hard. It's so hard that many churches, sometimes whole denominations, don't practice what Jesus preached.*

Have you ever been part of a church that had to carry out all the steps of Matthew chapter 18? If so, jot down and/or share the experience with others.

Have you ever had a friend or relative who has refused to repent of a sin? Explain how that has affected you.

Pastor Mike said:

*Here are the four stages that Jesus laid out for dealing with sin.*

Jot down and/or discuss the four stages that Jesus laid out for dealing with sin that people refuse to repent of.

Pastor Mike said:

*For the church to bind someone's sin on earth is like taking a roll of church duct tape and wrapping this sin in a person's hands and telling them, "This is stuck to you."*

Explain in your own words Pastor Mike's *church duct tape* analogy.

Pastor Mike said:

*That's why we do it. We love someone so much that we don't want them to stand before Jesus with the one thing that Jesus can't stand. Which is why we need Jesus' final words. At the end of this section, Jesus said something that pastors love to quote out of context. He said,* **"Truly I tell you that if two of you on earth agree about anything they ask for, it will be done for them by my Father in heaven. For where two or three gather in my name, there am I with them"** *(verses 19,20).* "When you're reaching out to someone you love and they're not changing and you feel like you can't do it, I'm right there," God says. . . . *Here's the big idea I want you to remember when you need to have a hard conversation:* God is here.

What are some examples of how the phrase "for where two or three gather in my name, there am I with them" has been taken out of context.

_____

_____

_____

_____

_____

_____

_____

Have your ever taken this phrase out of context? If so, explain what you thought the phrase meant?

# "More Than You Can Handle"
*1 Corinthians 10:1-13*

There's a rumor floating around the world of the Christian church, and I bet you've heard it before. The rumor is that God won't give you more than you can handle. Have you heard that?

Christians love to quote this idea when they see someone they love, a family member or a friend, who's overwhelmed with life. When finances or health problems or something in their personal lives is just more than they can handle, Christians love to quote this passage: "But don't forget that God has said he won't give you more than you can handle." It's an encouraging thing that's meant to be a spiritual boost, and it sounds nice. But there are two problems with the rumor.

Problem number one is that saying that to someone who feels like life is more than they can handle doesn't work. For example, if you feel like the next straw would break your back and I come up and smile and say, "Hey! Don't worry. God won't give you more than you can handle," instead of being incredibly comforted, you'd probably turn back in anger and say, "Well, this is way more than I can handle!"

Instead of loving God or trusting in God or being grateful to God, you might start to question God and maybe get angry or mad at God. The statement sounds nice on paper, but in practice it rarely does what we think it will do. It's not as encouraging. It's not as beautiful. It doesn't bring as much blessing as many Christians intend.

But that's not even the biggest problem. The biggest problem is not that the statement itself doesn't often work. The biggest problem is that this Bible passage isn't actually in the Bible. Did you know that? There are over 31,000 total verses in the Bible, and "God won't give you more than you can handle" is not one of them. There's something kind of like it in the New Testament in 1 Corinthians chapter 10, but I can guarantee you that when the apostle Paul wrote his words, he didn't mean this. He didn't mean that life and your burdens and the things you carry on your shoulders would not be more than you can handle. Because in context, the apostle Paul wasn't talking about pain or suffering or raising kids or mental health or financial struggles. In the context of when Paul wrote the words kind of like that phrase, he was talking about temptation.

In 1 Corinthians chapter 10, the apostle Paul was trying to share with some of his friends that God will never give one of his children *more temptation* than they can handle. The apostle Paul knew some people who were following Jesus who felt exactly like that. Like what they were facing was so strong and so powerful and their spirit was so weak that they just couldn't handle it. Kind of like the musical *Hamilton*. Have you ever heard of it? There's a scene in *Hamilton* where Alexander's being seduced by a married woman. He's a married man, and she's coming at him strong. It's a musical, so he goes on to rap a song where he talks about not knowing how to say no to this temptation. It's as if he knows it's wrong, but in the moment the temptation is so powerful he can't handle it; it's too strong.

I wonder if you've ever felt like that? Maybe you know the right thing to do or the Christian thing to do or the Bible thing to do, but there's this one thing that when you come face-to-face with it, you just don't know how to say no to it. And if that's you, you're the kind of person the apostle Paul was writing to. In fact, I think all of us are kind of that way; we're the kind of people the apostle Paul was addressing when he wrote those famous words in 1 Corinthians chapter 10.

You see, two thousand years ago, the apostle Paul started a church in a big Greek city called Corinth, and some of his friends were facing the kind of temptation that they didn't think they could handle.

If you've ever read the New Testament, you might know the story. Paul showed up in this big Greek city with all kinds of ideas and philosophies and religions, and he preached Jesus. He preached this really unique God named Jesus Christ who was so different than the Greek gods and goddesses of the Corinthian culture. He taught that Jesus was a God who didn't demand that you sacrifice to him or else; he was a God who sacrificed for you so that God could give you something else: an eternity with him, forgiveness, mercy, and grace. And when the Corinthians heard this, it changed their hearts. They thought religion was all about the quid pro quo: you do these things for the gods and they bless you. But here was a God of mercy and undeserved love, a God who would love you when you did bad things, a God who would bless you even though you were far from deserving it. That message, what Christians call the gospel, changed the Corinthians' hearts. And for 18 months, the apostle Paul preached that Jesus Christ was crucified, died on a cross, and rose from the dead for the forgiveness of sins. They loved it, and it changed them.

But one day Paul had to leave. He needed to go to other cities and tell more and more people about this Jesus. Almost as soon as Paul left, the temptation came, and it came strong. You see, the Corinthians lived in a culture that tempted them in some pretty massive and irresistible ways, and so you see the Corinthian dilemma. They thought, "I want to say no to this, but when everyone is pressuring me, when the temptation is so strong, what am I supposed to do?"

Let's look at Paul's words in context starting with 1 Corinthians 10:1: **"I do not want you to be ignorant of the fact, brothers and sisters, that our ancestors . . ."** Then he goes for ten verses with an Old Testament history lesson. Paul wants to remind his Corinthian friends of what happened in the first pages of the Bible. Maybe you know those stories, and maybe they're brand-new. In the next ten verses of 1 Corinthians chapter 10, Paul tells these very classic, Sunday school stories of what happened to God's Old Testament people. Then in verses 11 and 12, he reminds them why he's giving them this history lesson. He says, **"These things happened to them as examples and were written down as warnings for us, on whom the culmination of the ages has come. So, if you think you are standing firm, be careful that you don't fall!"**

Paul's saying to the Corinthians, "So you believe in God? Yeah, so did they. You pray to the true God? Well, so did they. Yet they combined that good worship with something else, and they fell. If you think somehow that because of your past, your present without repentance will be different, think again."

The reason the Old Testament is so long, the reason there are so many pages before we get to the story of Jesus, is because God wanted every person to know with all of these examples that sin is serious and idolatry must be left behind. He says, "If you think you're standing firm, if you think it couldn't possibly happen to a good person like you, be careful. Be careful that you don't fall."

If you think that a miracle or a moment from your past—a baptism or a confirmation—is your ticket and excuses any kind of behavior in the present, be careful that you don't fall. That's not how faith works. It's kind of like how the law works, right? If I get pulled over by a police officer and I've been smoking meth and there's a bunch of drugs in my trunk, I can't say to the cop, "You know what? I donated blood last year, and I gave to the Red Cross." I can't tell him about my past good works to excuse my present breaking of the law. No, what matters is the whole story and the whole picture, and that's what Paul's saying to us today. Praise God for your past, but take very seriously your present.

In love, I want to give you that warning. If you think you can hold on to this sin—and I know the temptation might be strong—but if you're starting to settle and you're giving up the fight and you're letting that sin seep into your heart and take root, be careful. Be careful that you don't fall away from the greatest gift of all time.

So that's Paul's warning: "Be careful, Corinthians. Be careful, Christians." But then he moves to his comfort. He says, **"No temptation has overtaken you except what is common to mankind"** (verse 13). This is the first of actually three comforting things that the apostle Paul wants to say, and he starts with this odd comfort. He says, "You know that temptation that seems like its way more than you can handle? Did you know that it's common to mankind? What you're facing is something that literally billions of Christians have faced before."

You're struggling financially, and you don't know if you can be generous. You are far from the first Christian who has ever been in that dilemma. Think of this: God has helped billions of people through that exact same temptation.

You're dating in a culture that doesn't date in God's way. There will be billions of brothers and sisters who are in the exact same position, and God is helping them make good choices and wait for long-term blessings.

Someone has hurt you in your past, and you find it really, really hard to forgive and not be bitter. God has helped tens of billions of people deal with that exact same temptation and forgive at the foot of the cross.

You find it hard to be pure or to stay sober or to trust God when life falls apart. Paul is saying that when you pray to God—"God, this is my temptation" —the one thing that God will never say is, "Huh. Man, wow. Never heard of that before. Can you give me a second? I'm going to Google that and see what I find." No, God says, "Oh yeah, that! Sure! I was just helping her and him and them." Billions of people deal with that exact same thing. You can pray to a God who's not ignorant about how to fix this. He has helped people just like you through temptation just like this. It's an incredible comfort that your temptation is common to mankind and your heavenly Father knows exactly how to fix it.

Then Paul moves to comfort number two. Same verse, next words: **"And God is faithful."** Here's my favorite part—not only is your temptation common, but your God is faithful. The word *faithful* means "dependable" or "reliable" or "trustworthy." God has made all these promises to you about dealing with temptation, and he has to keep his promises because he's God. So when you read the Bible and God makes you a promise, you can trust that he is faithful.

Let's say you're facing a temptation; you find it really, really hard to forgive someone in your life. But God is faithful. God has said, "I will never leave you; I will never forsake you. I will be with you always." So when you come face-to-face with that person and all those emotions start to swell up in your heart, who is faithfully by your side to help you? God. God is faithful. He said if you ask him for the Holy Spirit, the one who produces forgiveness and love and self-control, he will give it. Jesus once said, "If human fathers who are imperfect and sinful know how to give good gifts to our children, how much more will your Father in heaven give the Holy Spirit to those who ask him?" (see Matthew 7:11).

When you pray in the face of that temptation—"God, I don't think I can do this; I need your Spirit"—he's faithful and will give help. When you mess up and feel ashamed and guilty, God is faithful. First John 1:9 says, **"[God] is faithful and just and will forgive us our sins and purify us from all unrighteousness."** When you're struggling with regret, when you're living in the past, when you just can't get past that shame, God is faithful. At the cross of Jesus and because of the empty tomb of your risen Savior Jesus Christ, there is full forgiveness. You don't have to earn it; you don't have to work for it; you don't have to deserve it. God just gives it because he's faithful. He says, "Call upon me in the day of trouble. Cast all of your anxiety on me, and I will help you." Whether you struggle with self-control or shame, ask God. He is faithful.

But then Paul saves the best for last. The third and final comfort deserves a lot of attention. He says, **"He will not let you be tempted beyond what you can bear."** That's where that rumor comes from. **"But when you are tempted, he will also provide a way out so that you can endure it. Therefore, my dear friends, flee from idolatry"** (verses 13,14). I love this for so many reasons. Notice that Paul says, "When you are tempted, God will provide a way out." He says he will not let you be tempted beyond what you can bear. You will never face something that's so heavy that you can't handle it together.

Here's what Paul is saying. Think of it like a weight bench. You're lying on your back lifting the bar. You're trying to lift this temptation away from you and resist it, but do you know what the devil would love to do? He would love to put so much weight on the bar of your life that it just crushes your heart and soul, but God won't let him. God won't let you be tempted beyond what you can bear. God is holding him back. There's temptation that the devil would love to devour you with, but your heavenly Father loves you so much. He says, "Nope. I'm not going to let you do that."

God keeps the enemy on a leash so he can't devour you like he would like to. You won't be tempted beyond what you can bear. Instead, your Father in heaven will give you a way to endure it. And, actually, I bet you missed the power of that verse because I'm writing this in the northern part of the United States. Here in the North we don't know how many *you*s are in the word *you*. Do you know what I mean? If I'm talking to one person or two people or a larger group of people, I use the word *you*. But if we were doing church down in Alabama, it'd be a bit different, wouldn't it? I could speak to you or y'all individually or I could speak to all y'all, right? Did you know the Greek language of the New Testament is a lot more like Alabama than Wisconsin? If you could read Paul's original Greek, you could tell the difference between *you* (one person) or *all y'all* (together). In verse 13, Paul actually switches from the singular that he used in verse 12 to the plural. He starts in verse 12 by saying, "If you," singular, "think that you're standing firm, be careful that you," singular, "don't fall." But then here in verse 13, he switches it and says, "God won't give all y'all more than all y'all can handle."

What Paul's saying is that when you're trying to lift your temptation and it feels like it's more than you (singular) can handle, you're right. Often in life, God allows more temptation than you, as an individual Christian, can handle, but it's not too much for all y'all. If you live in a community with other people who worship Jesus, then you can handle it together. If you ask a brother in the faith to grab one end of the weight bar and a sister to grab the other one and a trusted friend to heave in the middle, there's no temptation that you can't endure if you rely on the family of God. That's the way that you flee temptations; that's the way that God provides a way out; that's the way that every Christian can endure it.

So the rumor is not exactly true. Sometimes life, sometimes even temptation, is more than you can handle individually. But if you reach out for help, you can handle it. In fact, I want you to highlight this: "God won't give you more temptation than all y'all can handle." If we would embrace the family of God. If we would leverage all those "one another" passages in the New Testament and pray for each other. If you could know me and I could know you and I could forgive the real you and you could encourage the real me, then there is no temptation that we would have to give in to. There is nothing that we would have to say yes to. We could honor God in all that we do because the truth is that God won't give you more than all y'all can handle.

I can tell you that I'm just learning how to do this too. I'm not sure if it's me or the church that I grew up in, but I didn't rely on the family of God for about 30 years of my life as a Christian. I would go to church every Sunday, and I would read my Bible in my bedroom. I would pray to Jesus every day, but I didn't really know people and people didn't know me. My temptation was mine, and my parents and my roommates and my friends didn't know about it. That was between me and God, and it crushed me. But then a few years ago, I found out how to do life together. I realized that God didn't bring churches and congregations together just so they could all worship Jesus individually in the same place. He did it so they could actually love and help one another.

At my last church, we started this ministry called small groups, where we actually started to do that. We would confess sins to each other and forgive each other in Jesus' name. We would be real with each other and bear burdens together and pray for each other in the midst of real temptation. And that's what I'm asking you to do today. Do you do life with people? Are you connected with fellow Christians? Could you join a group of Christians and actually be real—maybe for the first time in your life? Instead of getting crushed day after day by the temptation that is more than you can handle, would you let the family of God be the family of God? Because it works. No, we won't be perfect. Sure, you'll still need Jesus' forgiveness, but it works.

That's what happened to Latisha. There's a Christian woman named Latisha who lived in Guatemala, and one day she showed up to church pregnant, except she wasn't married. She knew she had done things backward according to Jesus' model of relationships, and she felt kind of embarrassed, kind of ashamed. But her church did the most amazing thing. One day, with Latisha's permission, the pastor, Roberto, called Latisha up front and put an arm around her shoulders—a visible reminder of Jesus' forgiveness and love for her mistake. Then he asked her church family a simple question: "So what are we going to do now? We can't change the past, so what are we going to do in the present?" That family of God responded as a family of God. One man raised his hand and said, "We're going to support Latisha." Another woman spoke for the group and said, "We're not going to gossip about her." Others offered to help financially with whatever Latisha needed. And when that baby came, the church family all pitched in and brought him a brand-new stroller and helped raise that little guy close to the family of God and, most important, close to Jesus himself.

Maybe the shame and guilt would have been the temptation that Latisha couldn't handle, but the church members grabbed the end of the weight bar. Maybe the temptation to gossip and treat her as some kind of worse sinner than they themselves would have been was more than they could handle, but they confessed and they pushed back together.

You will face temptation this week that is more than you can handle. But it's not more than all y'all can handle, so let's be real. Let's love one another. Let's gather at the foot of the cross of Jesus Christ. Let's grab an end of that bar. Let's do life as God intended, where all y'all do life together.

# Questions for Personal Reflection and/or Group Discussion

Pastor Mike spoke about a couple of problems with the phrase "more than you can handle." What are the problems he identified?

In 1 Corinthians 10:1-10, the apostle Paul gave a long history lesson filled with warnings. Pastor Mike said:
*Then in verses 11 and 12, he reminds them why he's giving them this history lesson.*

What were the reasons for giving the church in Corinth a lengthy history lesson?

Jot down and/or discuss what we need to earn from these warnings.

Pastor Mike said:

*So that's Paul's warning: "Be careful, Corinthians. Be careful, Christians." But then he moves to his comfort. He says,* **"No temptation has overtaken you except what is common to mankind"** *(verse 13). This is the first of actually three comforting things that the apostle Paul wants to say, and he starts with this odd comfort. He says, "You know that temptation that seems like its way more than you can handle? Did you know that it's common to mankind? What you're facing is something that literally billions of Christians have faced before."*

What comfort do you have when Paul says that "no temptation has overtaken you except what is common to mankind"?

Pastor Mike said:

*Then Paul moves to comfort number two. Same verse, next words:* **"And God is faithful."** *Here's my favorite part—not only is your temptation common, but your God is faithful. The word* faithful *means "dependable" or "reliable" or "trustworthy." God has made all these promises to you about dealing with temptation, and he has to keep his promises because he's God. So when you read the Bible and God makes you a promise, you can trust that he is faithful.*

What comfort do you have when Paul says that "God is faithful"?

Pastor Mike said:

*But then Paul saves the best for last. The third and final comfort deserves a lot of attention. He says,* **"He will not let you be tempted beyond what you can bear."** *. . . You will never face something that's so heavy that you can't handle it together.*

What comfort do you have when Paul says, "God will not let you be tempted beyond what you can bear"?

Jot down and/or share an example of a temptation from your own life in which God kept these three comforting promises.

Pastor Mike said:

*"God won't give all y'all more than all y'all can handle."*

Explain in your own words the contrast Pastor Mike makes between *y'all* and *all y'all*.

_____
_____
_____
_____
_____
_____

Pastor Mike said:

*You will face temptation this week that is more than you can handle. But it's not more than all y'all can handle, so let's be real. Let's love one another. Let's gather at the foot of the cross of Jesus Christ. Let's grab an end of that bar. Let's do life as God intended, where all y'all do life together.*

What are some examples of how the phrase "more than you can handle" has been taken out of context?

_____
_____
_____
_____

Have your ever taken this phrase out of context? If so, explain the *how* and the *why*.

# "Plans to Prosper You"

*Jeremiah 29:1-11*

My daughter jumped on a bandwagon recently. A couple of weeks ago, my littlest girl, Maya, had to do a project, and she told us as her family that her new all-time favorite Bible passage was Jeremiah 29:11. If you're new to the Bible and new to church, you might not know that this is a very popular and famous verse. If you've never seen it before, let me show you the words of Jeremiah 29:11: **"'I know the plans I have for you,' declares the Lord, 'plans to prosper you and not to harm you, plans to give you hope and a future.'"**

If you look at it, you can see why it's so popular. Here's one simple passage that says that God, the God of heaven and earth, has plans—not just plans for him or her or them—but plans for you. They're not plans to hurt you or condemn you or exclude you. They're plans to prosper you and to give you hope and to give you a future. Who wouldn't want more of that?

But can I burst your bubble? I think most Christians have taken that famous passage out of context. I think if the prophet Jeremiah was here and he would go to a Christian graduation or walk into a Christian home and look around, he would say, "Really? You quoted me now?" Because if you read the chapter that Jeremiah wrote it in and, in fact, the whole book called Jeremiah in the Old Testament, you would find out that it's not as warm and fuzzy as that passage sometimes feels.

Many Christians have actually given Jeremiah the prophet a nickname. Do you know what it is? He is called the weeping prophet. Apparently, his message was so difficult and so challenging and so many people didn't want to hear it that he would weep himself to sleep and say, "God, what am I doing? Why did you give me this message?" Which is not a common reaction in contemporary culture to that verse. In fact, before I did my writing on this passage, I breezed through the book of Jeremiah and skimmed the section and chapter headings. It's the longest book in the Bible—52 chapters—and if you would only read the headings and not even all the verses, you would find out that Jeremiah didn't have the easiest job. Half of his chapter headings could be names of heavy metal songs: "Cup of Wrath" and "Day of Disaster" and "Religion Is Worthless" and "Idolatress People." He had a hard, hard message that he preached for 40 years as a prophet.

In fact, not just the book, but chapter 29 itself was a hard message. Do you know when the original church heard Jeremiah speak the words that culminated in verse 11? Do you know how they reacted to it? "Get him!" They went in to arrest Jeremiah, put iron shackles around his neck, and drag him off to be tortured, if not killed, which I have never seen happen at a Christian graduation ceremony when Jeremiah 29:11 is quoted.

Now I'm not saying my daughter should love the passage any less. And I'm not saying you have to throw out all your coffee mugs or burn your Christian T-shirts that have Jeremiah 29:11 on them. I just want to make sure you turn to that passage at the right time in your life. If your life is pretty good right now, there are a whole lot of good Bible passages to read in this moment, but Jeremiah 29:11 is not your passage. If you're surrounded by family members whom you love, if you have good friends and your body's feeling pretty strong, there are amazing passages to recite and remember, but Jeremiah's not one of those passages. If your biggest struggle is worrying if it's going to rain on your weekend or your day off so you can get the boat out on the water, if you're just concerned about who the Green Bay Packer's backup quarterback is going to be for the next season, there are a lot of Bible passages that you could read, but please don't read this one. I want you to save this passage for the context that Jeremiah wrote it in.

Here's the context: When your life is really hard and it's kind of your fault, this is your passage. When now or in the future you find yourself at a spot in life that you never would have chosen when you were 18 years old and it's a mess and it's complicated and it's frustrating and it's partially your fault, I want you to stick a bookmark in Jeremiah 29:11 and read it until it gives you all the hope that you need.

It's for the day after you get your first DUI and you feel like a total idiot because you didn't need that drink and didn't need to drive and could have taken an Uber, but you didn't. You were proud. You didn't want to ask for help because it was embarrassing, so you pushed it and got pulled over. Now there are consequences. Now you have a court case, and they're going to take your license. Your reputation has been ruined, and maybe your name was even in the paper. That's the day, when you feel like a total loser, I want you to open your Bible and read this verse.

It's for the day when you're trying to find an apartment after your separation, after you couldn't make it work, after all the counseling. Here you are in this new place, and it just doesn't smell right or feel right and you miss your old bed. You miss seeing your dog, and you miss having your kids full time. You know that it was kind of his fault, but it was somewhat your fault. I want you to open your Bible in that apartment to Jeremiah 29:11.

It's for the day when you're in the doctor's office and there's another medication and another prescription and it's kind of your fault. All your life you'd heard what every doctor says—you should sleep this many hours and eat this many calories and exercise this many days a week—but you didn't. You thought you'd be the exception to God's rules of creation, and now your body is suffering the consequences.

I bet there are some major regrets that you have about life. And I know that all of us at some time in life are going to be in that place, so I want to prepare your heart today to plant this passage as a seed so it grows something beautiful. I don't want you to feel like you don't have hope or don't have a future or God doesn't have great plans to prosper you in years to come. Let's look at Jeremiah 29:11 in context.

Kind of near the end of the Old Testament, Jeremiah spends 40 years, his entire career, reaching out with the compassion of God, telling the people to repent. But they won't listen. So they go into exile during Jeremiah's lifetime, and that's the context.

Let's look at what happens in Jeremiah chapter 29: **"This is the text of the letter that the prophet Jeremiah sent from Jerusalem to the surviving elders among the exiles and to the priests, the prophets and all the other people Nebuchadnezzar had carried into exile from Jerusalem to Babylon. (This was after King Jehoiachin and the queen mother, the court officials and the leaders of Judah and Jerusalem, the skilled workers and the artisans had gone into exile from Jerusalem.) He entrusted the letter to Elasah son of Shaphan and to Gemariah son of Hilkiah, whom Zedekiah king of Judah sent to King Nebuchadnezzar in Babylon. It said, 'This is what the Lord Almighty, the God of Israel, says to all those I carried into exile from Jerusalem to Babylon'"** (verses 1-4).

Jeremiah the prophet is down in the city of Jerusalem, and he is with a king named Zedekiah, who will be the last king of Judah. There are a whole bunch of people who are still there, but most of the people aren't there anymore. They've been taken about 800 miles away to Babylon by King Nebuchadnezzar. In Babylon there are about 10,000 Israelites; a whole bunch of their prophets and their priests; and the old king, Jehoiachin. What you need to know is that in Babylon, all those prophets are claiming that they have this word from God for the people. The word they bring is, "It's going to be okay. Our God is a God of love and compassion and power, and he is just about to save us. Any day now, any week now, our God is going to crush King Nebuchadnezzar, and all of us will get to go back home to our beds and our homes and our backyards and our people."

Then these two messengers come to Babylon with a letter, and the letter is from Jeremiah the prophet. God spoke to him about the future of the exiles. Imagine the emotion of being dragged away in the middle of the night from your home to a whole other country. You're terrified. You want to go home desperately, and now here is God's decision. All the exiles gather around the messengers as they unroll the scroll and read the letter of what God has decided for his people.

Here's what God says: **"Build houses and settle down; plant gardens and eat what they produce. Marry and have sons and daughters; find wives for your sons and give your daughters in marriage, so that they too may have sons and daughters. Increase in number there; do not decrease. Also, seek the peace and prosperity of the city to which I have carried you into exile. Pray to the Lord for it, because if it prospers, you too will prosper"** (verses 5-7).

That sounds kind of nice, doesn't it? Plant and enjoy the produce and plan weddings and have babies and rock your grandkids in your arms. There's peace and there's prayer and there's prosperity, but did you catch the underlying message? You're not going home. There's a reason we don't plant a garden at a bus stop or remodel the hotel room we're staying in at Holiday Inn because we're not going to be there long. But God says, "Plant a garden and build a house and plan the wedding and raise the kid because you're not going home today or tomorrow or by the time your kid turns 18. Your kid is going to grow up and marry, and they're going to plan another wedding. Their kids are going to have kids because most of you will never get back home, no matter what those really warm and fuzzy prophets told you."

God speaks about those prophets in verses 8-10: **"This is what the Lord Almighty, the God of Israel, says: 'Do not let the**

**prophets and diviners among you deceive you. Do not listen to the dreams you encourage them to have. They are prophesying lies to you in my name. I have not sent them,' declares the L**ORD**. This is what the L**ORD** says: 'When seventy years are completed for Babylon, I will come to you and fulfill my good promise to bring you back to this place."** Seventy years. God says, "You wouldn't listen to me, and now there's a consequence. For 70 years I'm going to have to put you on this stair, this massive time-out, until you learn what it means to have no other gods and seek me with all of your hearts."

That might seem like some obscure historical story, but there's some really important lessons in those words for you and for me today. Let me just focus on two lessons that I see. Number one is to be aware of the "Pinterest prophets." In every age and in every generation, there will always be prophets—spiritual voices who speak in the name of God, in the name of Jesus, maybe even quoting a Bible passage—that tell you exactly what you want to hear. The prophets in Jeremiah's day did it. They said, "You're fine; God loves you. You know, you be you. You don't have to change, and God's going to save you." But it wasn't true. I want to warn you that that still exists today because pastors like me and priests and bloggers and Christian celebrities are human, so part of us really wants to be liked. None of us wants to weep at the end of the day that our work was in vain because no one wants to hear our message. There is a deep desire to compromise the things that God says. In fact, you can always find a church and a spiritual leader, a prophet, who will tell you exactly what you want to hear. If you go on Pinterest, you will find a lot of warm and fuzzy and flowery Bible passages, but do you know what you'll never find? "'Repent,' says Jesus." But that's what he taught.

If I would never confront you and ask you to change, if I would say that God loves you just as you are and you should stay that way, the only way that would be possible is if you were already

God and sinless. A faithful prophet, a faithful church, and a good pastor will always confront you in love. And you hope those conversations are few and far between. They are the exception and not the rule, but make sure you don't run away from those who love you and run to those who will tell you just what you always wanted them to say.

Life is complicated in these changing times. What will not help the family of God and grow the church of God are people who compromise the Word of God.

Here's the second lesson: That even if there are consequences, life's not over. I've thought about that—these people, the people of Israel, had been given so many chances. Jeremiah had begged and pleaded and wept with them for 40 years, and even though they had stiff-armed him for decades, what does God do? He still reaches out. He says he wants to bless their gardens and their families, and he wants them to pray to him. He hasn't closed his ear to them yet. God is still saying, "You might be mad about the place where I put you, but I still have plans for you." And that's a lesson for you to learn too. You might find yourself in a place in life and a consequence where God disciplines you. You can either choose to be bitter about that place, or you can lean on God and make it better.

I think about a guy whom I know from my church family who's in jail. It's kind of like his exile. Of course, he wishes he wasn't there. He wishes he could sleep in his own bed and eat good food, but he can't. But whenever I visit him and whenever I write to him, I always expect him to be kind of mad and angry and bitter about all of it. Do you know what I find instead? He wants to make it better. I come with my little Bible, ready with an encouraging, hopeful passage; and I always have to change the passage because his attitude surprises me. He says, "Pastor Mike, you won't believe these guys that I met in my cell block." And, "I started a Bible study. Three guys came to it, and six more said they're considering it, and one guy's thinking about being baptized. Pastor, we want to baptize him in the prison shower. Is that okay with Jesus?" Yes! That's okay with Jesus! This guy in jail gives me more joy because he's not bitter about the consequence; he's trying to make that place better.

We've gone through Jeremiah 29:1-10, so you know the context for verse 11 now: **"'For I know the plans I have for you,' declares the Lord, 'plans to prosper you and not to harm you, plans to give you hope and a future.'"** That passage can be even more powerful than it was before because now you know the "you" that Jeremiah is talking to. These are people in exile—people who made some major spiritual mistakes, people whose lives were filled with consequences. But what does God say? "I have plans for you, and I want to prosper you. I don't want to harm you. I want to give you hope and a future. Not you nice, beautiful, functional Christian families, but you who bring some major baggage and regret into church."

I love that; don't you? I know sometimes we smile and shake hands when we gather, but lots of us have lots of stuff going on. It might be an addiction. It might be multiple sexual partners in our pasts. It might be the divorce and the anger that is in our hearts. It might be alcohol. It might be food. It might be self-righteousness. It might be control issues. We've all got something, but despite the mess, Jeremiah still has this message: God has plans for us. Life isn't over yet. God is a God of ridiculous grace and incredible patience, and it's for you. Not for him or them or those people who are better than you, but for you. Even if you feel like you're in Babylon.

Despite our sins, Jeremiah says that God still has plans. He's not done with us yet. There's hope. He's not finished with your story. There's a future. You might think that you lost your chance, like the people in exile, but God says, "No, no, no."

Do you know how I know that? Because I read the context. If you would do the hard work of reading through Jeremiah, all the cup of wrath and day of disaster and worthless religion, do you know what you would find? You would find this passage in Jeremiah chapter 23: **"'The days are coming,' declares the Lord, 'when I will raise up for David a righteous Branch, a King who will reign wisely and do what is just and right in the land. In his days Judah will be saved and Israel will live in safety. This is the name by which he will be called: The Lord Our Righteous Savior'"** (verses 5,6). Want to guess who that is? A Branch from David's family tree? A King of Israel who wouldn't try to fill his pockets and hold on to his sins but would do what is just and right and wise? Someone who would lead God's people, not into slavery and exile but into salvation and safety? Whose name would be the Lord Our Righteous Savior? That's a prophecy about Jesus.

Jesus is the reason that we can say, "Still." Because Jesus went to a cross, there is still hope. Because Jesus rose from the dead, there is still forgiveness. And if you believe in Jesus, no matter what happened last night, you can wake up every morning and say, "Still." God still has plans. He still wants to prosper you and me. He still wants to give us a great future.

I talked to this guy from my church this past week who wants to bring his friends to worship. He's part of a recovery community, and he's escaped some pretty hard drug abuse in his past. All of his friends have used meth and heroin, and he wants them to come, but he said, "Pastor, I don't want to trick them. I don't want them to think if they come here addiction is just gone and one church service or one prayer or just believing in Jesus makes everything better. I want them to come for the right reasons. So what should I tell them?" Maybe Jeremiah 29:11 is what he should tell them: that there is hope for addicts and there's a future, even if there are consequences because of the past. Jesus might not bring you home out of Babylon; there might be a time you have to live with—maybe even 70 years—of consequences. Yet, because of Jesus, there is still salvation.

That's what I want to tell you. I can't promise you that going to a church will fix your marriage. And I can't promise that a church can fix the addiction or get you out of debt or make your family functional again. I hope it can—the Bible is powerful and effective—but here's what I can promise you. Even if you're a mess and even if you've messed a thousand things up, there's still hope for the people of God. This is our calling card. Not to fix lives but to fix them forever. There's a community out there who thinks that churches are where good church people get a little bit better, but it's not. It's where messed-up people find hope and a future.

When you're messed up and you mess up, you go to church, okay? And when you're embarrassed and you think church people are the last people you want to see, they're the first people you should run to because they will bring you to Jesus. In Jesus there's always hope.

That's what I'm going to say on graduation day. My little Maya is only in third grade right now; she's got a lot of years to go. But if they ask me to be the graduation speaker, I know what I'm going to talk about. Can I tell you? I'm going to choose for my passage Jeremiah 29:11, and here's what I'm going to say:

"God has a powerful word for us today. But it's not for you, Mr. Valedictorian, with the fancy little tassel on your hat." I'll try not to be bitter about it when I actually preach it. "And it's not for you, all you people who graduated with high honors and have great college plans for your future. It's not for you, Mom and Dad. I see you holding hands with your perfect Instagram marriage and your cheesy potatoes waiting at home for the graduation party. It's not for you who have cakes waiting for you with your face somehow photoshopped on top of it. No, there are great Bible passages for you, but not this one. This one is for you way in the back who doesn't get to walk the stage for graduation because you did something really stupid on prom night. This is for you. And for you, Mom and Dad, who couldn't even keep it civil after the divorce, even at your kid's graduation. This is for you, all you older brothers and sisters who thought you were going to change the world when you were 18 and you found out you couldn't even change yourself. All of you who woke up this morning and didn't like what you saw in the mirror and didn't like yourself or your life, I've got a passage for you. It goes like this: **"'For I know the plans I have for you," declares the Lord, "plans to prosper you and not to harm you, plans to give you hope and a future.'"** That's Jeremiah 29:11 in context. Amen."

# Questions for Personal Reflection and/or Group Discussion

Pastor Mike said:
*Do you know when the original church heard Jeremiah speak the words that culminated in verse 11?*

Describe the historical setting for this phrase, both the real-life situation for Jeremiah as well as for God's people.

Pastor Mike said:

*I want you to save this passage for the context that Jeremiah wrote it in. Here's the context: When your life is really hard and it's kind of your fault, this is your passage. When now or in the future you find yourself at a spot in life that you never would have chosen when you were 18 years old and it's a mess and it's complicated and it's frustrating and it's partially your fault, I want you to stick a bookmark in Jeremiah 29:11 and read it until it gives you all the hope that you need.*

In the context of this passage, are there any examples in your life where you made a mess of things?

How does this passage provide comfort for the messes in our lives?

Pastor Mike said:

*Here's what God says:* **"Build houses and settle down; plant gardens and eat what they produce. Marry and have sons and daughters; find wives for your sons and give your daughters in marriage, so that they too may have sons and daughters. Increase in number there; do not decrease. Also, seek the peace and prosperity of the city to which I have carried you into exile. Pray to the Lord for it, because if it prospers, you too will prosper"** *(verses 5-7).*

God's way of prospering us doesn't always align with our idea of prospering. Do you have any examples in your life of how God prospered you in a way that you would never have dreamed of?

Pastor Mike said:

*If you would do the hard work of reading through Jeremiah, all the cup of wrath and day of disaster and worthless religion, do you know what you would find? You would find this passage in Jeremiah chapter 23.*

Refer to Jeremiah 23:5,6. What is the ultimate "plan to prosper us"?

What are some examples of how the phrase "plans to prosper you" has been taken out of context?

Have your ever taken this phrase out of context? If so, explain what you thought and why?

# What Else Is Out of Context?

In this section, we will look at another four verses or phrases that are often taken out of context. But instead of explaining how they've been taken out of context, as Pastor Mike did, the goal is to help you discover the context and meaning for yourself. By doing so, you will become more confident in understanding the meaning of the words and phrases you read in the Bible.

## "Money Is a Root of All Kinds of Evil"

This phrase paints a rather negative picture of money. In the King James translation of the Bible, there are several references to money as being "filthy lucre." Filthy money—that's certainly a negative description, don't you think? So does the Bible teach that money is a root cause of evil in the world?

Let's see what the Bible says about money.

In the NIV11 translation of the Bible, the word *money* occurs 112 times (60 times in the Old Testament and 52 times in the New Testament). In addition, there are many more references to money using similar words such as *gold, silver, coins, possessions,* etc.

### *Old Testament*

In Genesis chapters 42-45, there's the story of Jacob and his 12 sons. In chapter 42, there's a severe famine in the land of Israel, so Jacob sends 10 of his sons to Egypt to buy grain. Their brother Joseph, whom the other brothers had sold into slavery years earlier, had been blessed by God to become the number-two leader in Egypt and in charge of the grain. Read chapters 42-45 and comment on how money is described and used. Is it positive, negative, or neutral?

In Genesis 47:13-26, there's an account of Joseph acquiring money for Pharaoh. Read these verses and comment on how money is described and used. Is it positive, negative, or neutral?

In 2 Kings chapter 12, we meet King Joash, one of the few faithful kings in the nation of Judah. Read this chapter and comment on how money is described and used. Is it positive, negative, or neutral?

In Nehemiah chapter 5, Nehemiah reacts to a situation that has developed among the people who are working to rebuild the walls of Jerusalem. Read this chapter and comment on how money is described and used. Is it positive, negative, or neutral?

King Solomon wrote in Ecclesiastes 5:10: **"Whoever loves money never has enough; whoever loves wealth is never satisfied with their income. This too is meaningless."** What is Solomon saying about money?

---

### New Testament

In his Sermon on the Mount, Jesus said: **"No one can serve two masters. Either you will hate the one and love the other, or you will be devoted to the one and despise the other. You cannot serve both God and money"** (Matthew 6:24). What was the point Jesus was making? (Hint: read this verse in its context of Matthew chapter 6. Also, check out Luke 16:13-15, where Jesus spoke the same words to a different audience.)

Jesus taught multiple parables that involved money. One of the more familiar ones is the parable of the bags of gold (Matthew 25:14-30). Read this parable and comment on how money is described and used. Is it positive, negative, or neutral?

Another parable taught by Jesus was the parable of the good Samaritan (Luke 10:25-34). Read this parable and comment on how money is described and used. Is it positive, negative, or neutral?

One account that gives multiple perspectives on money is found in Luke 21:1-4: **"As Jesus looked up, he saw the rich putting their gifts into the temple treasury. He also saw a poor widow put in two very small copper coins. 'Truly I tell you,' he said, 'this poor widow has put in more than all the others. All these people gave their gifts out of their wealth; but she out of her poverty put in all she had to live on.'"** What are your takeaways on money from these verses?

Before we look at the specific verse—"money is a root of all kinds of evil"—summarize how money is described and used in the Bible sections we've just looked at.

How is money described as a positive?

How is it viewed as a negative?

How is it characterized as neutral?

Let's now take a look at the verse that's often taken out of context. It's found in 1 Timothy 6:10: **"Money is a root of all kinds of evil. Some people, eager for money, have wandered from the faith and pierced themselves with many griefs."**

That's what it says, right? If you open your Bible to this passage, what do you notice? Four words are omitted from the beginning of this verse that totally change the meaning of the verse.

**"*For the love of* money is a root of all kinds of evil. . . ."** It is the *love of* and *an obsession for* money is a root of all kinds of evil.

There are many examples in the Bible of real-life people who loved money. Jot down and/or discuss as many as you can think of.

Then look up the following Bible verses to see how many you thought of and some that you may not have. Can you think of any others who aren't mentioned in these verses?

Joshua 7:1-26:

1 Samuel 8:1-3:

Luke 16:13-15:

Luke 16:19-28:

Luke 18:18-25:

Luke 19:1-10:

John 12:1-6:

Acts 5:1-11:

Acts 24:1-27:

"Money is a root of all kinds of evil" is indeed stated in the Bible, but without the four words that precede this phrase, it ends up being taken out of context—both the immediate context of the verse and the wider context of how "money" is described and used throughout the Bible.

## "I Can Do All Things Through Christ Who Strengthens Me"

Christian athlete and NBA star Steph Curry has probably done more to highlight this verse (Philippians 4:13) than any other person. He references it often. It serves as the foundation for his motivational talks to other athletes. He even has the verse inscribed on his court shoes and has used a Sharpie to do so since his college days at Davidson. Curry even switched shoe companies when his former shoe company said he couldn't write this Bible verse on "their" shoes.

In a 2018 interview with ESPN, Curry elaborated on his use of Philippians 4:13:

> "It's a mantra that I live by and something that drives me every single day," Curry said. "It'll hopefully inspire people to find something that drives them, whether that's a verse or some other motivating force that keeps you hungry and keeps you driven. That's mine, and you can pick whatever yours is and let that drive you, too, as you continue with basketball or whatever field you're in in your life" (Ananth Pandian, "Steph Curry Explains Why He Writes Philippians 4:13 on His Sneakers," *USA Today Sports*, March 21, 2018).

Are Curry and other athletes, professionals, businesspeople, students, and many more using this verse in context or out of context? It will be helpful first to understand the circumstances and setting of both the author and the audience.

Around A.D. 60, the apostle Paul was arrested in Jerusalem and faced trial in the coastal town of Caesarea before Governor Festus. During the trial, Paul appealed his case to Caesar in Rome. As a result of his appeal, Paul was taken by ship to Rome. Upon arriving . . .

> **"Three days later he called together the local Jewish leaders. When they had assembled, Paul said to them, 'My brothers, although I have done nothing against our people or against the customs of our ancestors, I was arrested in Jerusalem and handed over to the Romans. They examined me and wanted to release me, because I was not guilty of any crime deserving death. The Jews objected, so I was compelled to make an appeal to Caesar. I certainly did not intend to bring any charge against my own people.' . . . For two whole years Paul stayed there in his own rented house and welcomed all who came to him. He proclaimed the kingdom of God and taught about the Lord Jesus Christ—with all boldness and without hindrance!"** (Acts 28:17-19,30,31).

During these two years, Paul wrote several letters to several churches. These letters are known as the Prison Epistles. One of the letters was written to the church in Philippi.

Paul first visited Philippi during his second missionary journey (Acts 16) and again on his third missionary journey (Acts 20). He enjoyed a close relationship with this congregation. In fact, even though the city of Philippi had a lower economic status, the church supported Paul's missionary work financially. When the church learned that Paul was under house arrest in Rome, they sent a man by the name of Epaphroditus to Rome with financial support for Paul. When Epaphroditus returned to Philippi, he took with him Paul's letter to the Philippians.

With this background information (which can be found in any Bible commentary or in an online search), let's look at Philippians chapter 4, the immediate context for this verse: **"Therefore, my brothers and sisters, you whom I love and long for, my joy and crown, stand firm in the Lord in this way, dear friends!"** (verse 1).

What is Paul encouraging the Christians in Philippi to do?

Why? (The word "therefore" is a clue to read the end of chapter 3 to answer this question.)

"I plead with Euodia and I plead with Syntyche to be of the same mind in the Lord. Yes, and I ask you, my true companion, help these women since they have contended at my side in the cause of the gospel, along with Clement and the rest of my co-workers, whose names are in the book of life" (verses 2,3).

We don't know what the issue was between Euodia and Syntyche, but there appears to be some conflict and/or discontent.

"Rejoice in the Lord always. I will say it again: Rejoice! Let your gentleness be evident to all. The Lord is near. Do not be anxious about anything, but in every situation, by prayer and petition, with thanksgiving, present your requests to God. And the peace of God, which transcends all understanding, will guard your hearts and your minds in Christ Jesus. Finally, brothers and

**sisters, whatever is true, whatever is noble, whatever is right, whatever is pure, whatever is lovely, whatever is admirable—if anything is excellent or praiseworthy—think about such things. Whatever you have learned or received or heard from me, or seen in me—put it into practice. And the God of peace will be with you"** (verses 4-9).

What is Paul encouraging his readers NOT TO DO?

_____

_____

_____

_____

What is he encouraging them TO DO?

_____

_____

_____

_____

What is the relationship between the "not do" and the "do"?

_____

_____

_____

_____

_____

**"I rejoiced greatly in the Lord that at last you renewed your concern for me. Indeed, you were concerned, but you had no opportunity to show it. I am not saying this because I am in need, for I have learned to be content whatever the circumstances. I know what it is to be in need, and I know what it is to have plenty. I have learned the secret of being content in any and every situation, whether well fed or hungry, whether living in plenty or in want"** (verses 10-12).

These verses set the context for verse 13 to follow. What has Paul learned to do in his circumstances, his everyday life?

**"I can do all this through him who gives me strength"** (verse 13).

In light of verses 10-12—the immediate context of this verse—what is the "this" that Paul refers to?

**"Yet it was good of you to share in my troubles. Moreover, as you Philippians know, in the early days of your acquaintance with the gospel, when I set out from Macedonia, not one church shared with me in the matter of giving and receiving, except you only; for even when I was in Thessalonica, you sent me aid more than once when I was in need. Not that I desire your gifts; what I desire is that more be credited to your account. I have received full payment and have more than enough. I am amply supplied, now that I have received from Epaphroditus the gifts you sent. They are a fragrant offering, an acceptable sacrifice, pleasing to God. And my God will meet all your needs according to the riches of his glory in Christ Jesus. To our God and Father be glory for ever and ever. Amen"** (verses 14-20).

What words does Paul, in these verses, use to repeat the main point of this chapter, namely that "I can be content through him who gives me strength no matter what my circumstances are in life"?

_____

_____

_____

Out of context, people use the phrase "I can do all this through him who gives me strength" in the following ways:
- I can do anything that I set my mind to.
- I can be successful at whatever I do.
- I can be the best in my profession or field.
- I can achieve wealth and fame when I choose to be my best.

In context, we can say with Paul, "I can be content in whatever my circumstances are because of the strength Christ gives me."

## "Be Still and Know That I Am God"

If you do a web search on this popular phrase and click on "images" in the search results, you will find hundreds and hundreds of images that all look similar. In addition to the words of Psalm 46:10, the background images chosen are of serene landscapes, quiet waters, peaceful sunrises, and people quietly resting. The images suggest that each of us needs to take a deep breath, let go, and give everything to God. The images suggest that we should sit quietly before our God, read his Word, and spend time in prayer. "Be still and know that I am God."

It's true that these are attitudes and actions that Christians aspire to. The Bible speaks about these attitudes and actions elsewhere but . . . not in Psalm 46. Psalm 46 is not about peace and quietness. It's about war. And when God says, **"Be still and know that I am God,"** he isn't talking to you and me. He's shouting at his enemies.

Let's look at the context of Psalm 46. The literary form is Hebrew poetry. In each verse the content of the first line is repeated and expanded upon in the second line.

The authors of this psalm are the sons (descendants) of Korah. Korah was a rebel at the time of Moses along with Dathan, Abiriam, and On. The four of them recruited 250 other men to join them in rebellion against Moses. God dealt with that rebellion swiftly and completely by opening up the earth and swallowing them (Numbers 16).

But God had a different plan for the descendants of Korah. The faithful prophet Samuel came from Korah's line. Other descendants of Korah became doorkeepers and custodians of the tabernacle (1 Chronicles 9). Others served in David's army (1 Chronicles 12). Of greatest significance, however, were the descendants of Korah who became the leaders of choral and instrumental music in the tabernacle. There are 11 psalms (songs) attributed to the sons of Korah, Psalm 46 being one of them.

Some Bible scholars believe that this psalm was written during the time of the Assyrian siege on Jerusalem during the reign of King Hezekiah. Outside the city walls of Jerusalem were 185,000 Assyrian soldiers, led by Sennacherib, the king of Assyria. One night the angel of the Lord visited the Assyrian camp. The next morning the citizens of Jerusalem awoke to find 185,000 *dead* Assyrian soldiers. Keep that in mind as we consider this psalm.

**"God is our refuge and strength,**
  **an ever-present help in trouble.**
**Therefore we will not fear, though the earth give way**
  **and the mountains fall into the heart of the sea,**
**though its waters roar and foam**
  **and the mountains quake with their surging"** (verses 1-3).

What is the promise that God makes to his people who love and serve him?

What is he protecting his people from?

And what is the result? (Note the word "therefore.")

"There is a river whose streams make glad the city of God,
   the holy place where the Most High dwells.
God is within her, she will not fall;
   God will help her at break of day.
Nations are in uproar, kingdoms fall;
   he lifts his voice, the earth melts.
The Lord Almighty is with us;
   the God of Jacob is our fortress" (verses 4-7).

For God's Old Testament people, what is the city of God, the holy place where God dwells?

What is going on around the city of God?

> "Come and see what the Lord has done,
>   the desolations he has brought on the earth.
> He makes wars cease
>   to the ends of the earth.
> He breaks the bow and shatters the spear;
>   he burns the shields with fire" (verses 8,9).

What did God do to those who raged against him and his people?

> "He says, 'Be still, and know that I am God;
>   I will be exalted among the nations,
>   I will be exalted in the earth.'
> The Lord Almighty is with us;
>   the God of Jacob is our fortress" (verses 10,11).

The context of verse 10 is war. In this war God protects his people by going out on the battlefield to confront his enemies. There he defeats them.

What is the weapon that he uses to defeat them?

What does God tell his enemies to do, and what does he promise them will happen?

_____

_____

_____

_____

The immediate context of Psalm 46 involves God's Old Testament people living in the nation of Judah where God protected his people and defeated their enemies. There is also a wider context of Scripture in which we learn how our God has defeated our enemies and established his church, the city of God.

God's Son, Jesus, defeated sin and Satan and the evil in this world. He defeated the unholy trio with his perfect life and sacrificial death. And, with his resurrection from the grave, Jesus established his church. One day, the perfect fulfillment of this psalm will bring about peace and joy and a quiet stillness for all eternity. Jesus' victory will be ours to enjoy in the new heavens and the new earth.

The reformer Martin Luther composed a hymn based on Psalm 46. He captured the context of this psalm in these lyrics, as they relate to us today and our anticipation of Jesus' return on the Last Day:

> A mighty fortress is our God, a trusty shield and weapon;
> He helps us free from every need that has us now o'er-taken.
> The old evil foe now means deadly woe;
> Deep guile and great might are his dread arms in fight;
> On earth is not his equal.

With might of ours can naught be done; soon were our loss effected.
But for us fights the valiant one whom God himself elected.
You ask, "Who is this?" Jesus Christ it is, the almighty Lord.
And there's no other God; he holds the field forever.

Though devils all the world should fill, all eager to devour us,
We tremble not, we fear no ill; they shall not overpower us.
This world's prince may still scowl fierce as he will,
He can harm us none. He's judged; the deed is done!
One little word can fell him.

The Word they still shall let remain, nor any thanks have for it;
He's by our side upon the plain with his good gifts and Spirit.
And do what they will—hate, steal, hurt, or kill—
Though all may be gone, our victory is won;
The kingdom's ours forever!

Out of context, the phrase "be still and know that I am God" is about peace and calm.

In context, it is about war that God wages to defeat the enemies of sin, the world, and Satan. However, the result of the war that Jesus waged against our enemies does indeed bring about peace and calm for those who are in Christ.

## "Forgive and Forget"

This phrase does not occur in the Bible. There's no place where God directs his people to "forgive and forget." So where does this phrase come from? The question we want to consider is: Although the phrase doesn't actually occur in the Bible, does the biblical text support the concept of this phrase?

"Forgive and forget"—out of context or in context? We'll take a look at several sections of the Bible that seem to suggest the idea of forgiving and forgetting.

## Isaiah 43

Let's first take a look at Isaiah chapter 43. To understand what is said in this chapter, it's important to know the historical context of Isaiah's ministry. Isaiah was called to be a prophet during the time of King Hezekiah, the king of Judah, the Southern Kingdom of God's people. This occurred around 700 B.C.

By the time of Isaiah's ministry, the Northern Kingdom of Israel had already been invaded and destroyed by the Assyrians. In 722 B.C., 22 years earlier, the Assyrians laid siege to the Northern Kingdom's capital city of Samaria for three years. When the city fell, the Assyrians took captive the remaining people. The Northern Kingdom was no more.

Around 700 B.C., the Assyrians marched on Jerusalem to destroy it as well. God intervened by sending an angel one night to eliminate the Assyrian army, all 185,000 of them. (See also the section on "Be Still and Know That I Am God.") The Southern Kingdom of Judah would be spared from the Assyrian threat.

However, Judah was not without blame either. Isaiah's message was that because of Judah's disobedience of God, their lack of concern for their spiritual lives, and their lack of trust in the power of God, Judah would also face a sad ending, this time at the hands of the Babylonians. Jerusalem would fall to the Babylonians in 586 B.C.

The first 39 chapters of Isaiah address the current events of his time, with chapter 39 ending with Jerusalem being spared from the Assyrian siege. Also, in chapter 39, Isaiah references the future collapse of Judah at the hands of the Babylonians, which wouldn't occur for more than another one hundred-plus years.

Isaiah chapter 40 fast-forwards and begins with the reality that the Babylonians had already come to power and taken Judah captive. Isaiah looks ahead to the day that God would deliver his people from the Babylonians. God would raise up a new ruler, Cyrus, who would allow the Jews to return to Jerusalem. This would occur in 538 B.C.

In addition to describing the future history of God's people, Isaiah introduces a future someone known as the "Great Servant of the Lord." These are prophecies about Jesus, whom God sent to fulfill his promise of forgiving sins made to Moses on Mt. Sinai: **"The Lord, the Lord, the compassionate and gracious God, slow to anger, abounding in love and faithfulness, maintaining love to thousands, and forgiving wickedness, rebellion and sin. Yet he does not leave the guilty unpunished"** (Exodus 34:6,7).

These prophecies about Jesus are found throughout the second half of the book of Isaiah. Look up each passage in your Bible and summarize what Isaiah tells us.

Isaiah 42:1-7:

Isaiah 49:1-7:

Isaiah 50:4-11:

Isaiah 52:13–53:12:

Isaiah 61:1-3:

Isaiah 63:1-6:

With the historical context in mind and the prophecies about the future "Great Servant of the Lord," let's look at Isaiah chapter 43:

**"This is what the L**ORD** says—
your Redeemer, the Holy One of Israel:
'For your sake I will send to Babylon
and bring down as fugitives all the Babylonians,
in the ships in which they took pride'"** (verse 14).

Even though God's people were disobedient, what does God declare himself to be? What is the significance of God's self-description?

What Else Is Out of Context? | 107

What does he say that he is going to do with Babylon?

"'I am the Lord, your Holy One,
   Israel's Creator, your King.'
This is what the Lord says—
   he who made a way through the sea,
   a path through the mighty waters,
who drew out the chariots and horses,
   the army and reinforcements together,
and they lay there, never to rise again,
   extinguished, snuffed out like a wick:
'Forget the former things;
   do not dwell on the past.
See, I am doing a new thing!
   Now it springs up; do you not perceive it?
I am making a way in the wilderness
   and streams in the wasteland.
The wild animals honor me,
   the jackals and the owls,
because I provide water in the wilderness
   and streams in the wasteland,
to give drink to my people, my chosen,
   the people I formed for myself
   that they may proclaim my praise'" (verses 15-21).

What do each of the following descriptions/names for God emphasize?

"Lord":

"Holy One":

"Israel's Creator":

"Your King":

What historical events does God reference? Why does he do that?

In verse 21, God gives the reason why he chose the Israelites to be his people? What is that reason?

**"'Yet you have not called on me, Jacob,
  you have not wearied yourselves for me, Israel.
You have not brought me sheep for burnt offerings,
  nor honored me with your sacrifices.
I have not burdened you with grain offerings
  nor wearied you with demands for incense.
You have not bought any fragrant calamus for me,
  or lavished on me the fat of your sacrifices.
But you have burdened me with your sins
  and wearied me with your offenses'"** (verses 22-24).

How did God's people respond to God's gracious choice to call them his people?

**"I, even I, am he who blots out
your transgressions, for my own sake,
and remembers your sins no more"** (verse 25).

God says that he forgives sins "for my own sake." What does that mean? (Hint: revisit Exodus 34:6,7.)

 

 

 

God doesn't say that he "forgives and forgets." He says that "he forgives and chooses not to remember." What is the difference between "forgetting" and "choosing not to remember"?

 

 

 

Is there anything in this passage that says that we, as God's creation, are able to do what he does? Why is that distinction important?

### *Jeremiah 31*

The prophet Jeremiah, who lived during the Babylonian conquest of the Southern Kingdom of Judah, was told by God something similar to what Isaiah prophesied.

**"'The days are coming,' declares the Lord,**
  **'when I will make a new covenant**
**with the people of Israel**
  **and with the people of Judah.**
**It will not be like the covenant**
  **I made with their ancestors**
**when I took them by the hand**
  **to lead them out of Egypt,**
**because they broke my covenant,**
  **though I was a husband to them,'**
**declares the Lord"** (verses 31,32).

What was the "old" covenant?

How did the Israelites respond to that covenant?

"'This is the covenant I will make with the people of Israel
 after that time,' declares the Lord.
'I will put my law in their minds
 and write it on their hearts.
I will be their God,
 and they will be my people.
No longer will they teach their neighbor,
 or say to one another, "Know the Lord,"
because they will all know me,
 from the least of them to the greatest,'
declares the Lord.
'For I will forgive their wickedness
 and will remember their sins no more'"** (verses 33,34).

What is the "new" covenant that God would make with his people?

What would God do in order to forgive their wickedness?

Again, God doesn't say he will forget their sins. He says he will remember them no more. What enables God to remember our sins no more?

These verses are quoted by the writer to the Hebrews in the New Testament. Read Hebrews chapter 8 and note the relationship of what God says through Jeremiah and Jesus serving as a priest of the new covenant.

### *Psalm 103*

King David wrote Psalm 103. In it he paints a picture of what God has done to forgive sins and the reason why he forgives sins.

**"Praise the Lord, my soul;**
  **all my inmost being, praise his holy name.**
**Praise the Lord, my soul,**
  **and forget not all his benefits—**
**who forgives all your sins**
  **and heals all your diseases,**
**who redeems your life from the pit**
  **and crowns you with love and compassion,**
**who satisfies your desires with good things**
  **so that your youth is renewed like the eagle's.**
**The Lord works righteousness**
  **and justice for all the oppressed.**
**He made known his ways to Moses,**
  **his deeds to the people of Israel"** (verses 1-7).

The psalmist David refers to how God "made known his ways to Moses." It is a reference once again to God's promise in Exodus 34:6,7. It's a reference worth committing to memory.

Then David summarizes the promise of God to Moses:

**"The Lord is compassionate and gracious,**
  **slow to anger, abounding in love.**
**He will not always accuse,**
  **nor will he harbor his anger forever;**
**he does not treat us as our sins deserve**
  **or repay us according to our iniquities.**
**For as high as the heavens are above the earth,**
  **so great is his love for those who fear him;**
**as far as the east is from the west,**

**so far has he removed our transgressions from us"** (verses 8-12).

Again, how has God removed our transgressions from us? Does he forget them or not?

---

The prophet Micah reflects the same truth about the nature of God and how he deals with human sin and disobedience. These verses are from Micah chapter 7:

**"Who is a God like you,**
  **who pardons sin and forgives the transgression**
  **of the remnant of his inheritance?**
**You do not stay angry forever**
  **but delight to show mercy.**
**You will again have compassion on us;**
  **you will tread our sins underfoot**
  **and hurl all our iniquities into the depths of the sea.**
**You will be faithful to Jacob,**
  **and show love to Abraham,**
**as you pledged on oath to our ancestors**
  **in days long ago"** (verses 18-20).

What is the unique analogy that Micah uses regarding how God deals with sin and disobedience?

What comfort and confidence do you experience when you contemplate Micah's analogy?

These sections of the Bible talk about God's forgiveness and the linkage between God's Old Testament promise to Moses on Mt. Sinai and the fulfillment of that promise in the life and work of God's Son, Jesus Christ.

Out of context, "forgive and forget" suggests that we humans can do what the Bible only attributes to God. Encouraging people to "forgive and forget" hurtful and horrible deeds done to them by others can undermine the biblical concepts of forgiveness and reconciliation.

In context, God chooses not to remember our sins any longer because they have been forgiven in the blood of Jesus. Because of Jesus, we are not only forgiven but also reconciled (restored) to God.

Jot down or share an experience of when you were wronged and how you reacted to the situation.

Were you able to forgive the person?

Were you able to be reconciled to the person? Why or why not?

Dr. Martin Luther King once said:

"Forgiveness does not mean ignoring what has been done or putting a false label on an evil act. It means, rather, that the evil act no longer remains as a barrier to the relationship. Forgiveness is a catalyst creating the atmosphere necessary for a fresh start and a new beginning. It is the lifting of a burden or the cancelling of a debt. The words 'I will forgive you, but I'll never forget what you've done' never explain the real nature of forgiveness. Certainly, one can never forget, if that means erasing it totally from his mind. But when we forgive, we forget in the sense that the evil deed is no longer a mental block impeding a new relationship. Likewise, we can never say, 'I will forgive you, but I won't have anything further to do with you.' Forgiveness means reconciliation, a coming together again. Without this, no man can love his enemies. The degree to which we are able to forgive determines the degree to which we are able to love our enemies" (Martin Luther King Jr., *A Gift of Love*, Beacon Press, 2012).

Jot down and/or discuss how King's words relate to the Bible sections we've considered on forgiveness.

# Conclusion

One of the key principles in understanding the Bible's meaning of any particular word, verse, section, or book of the Bible is context.

Taking statements of the Bible out of context can lead either to an incomplete or incorrect understanding of God's truth. Understanding them in context gives a richer understanding and appreciation for what God's words say and mean.

On the previous pages, we looked at and dug deep into many sections of the Bible. Were you intimidated? Maybe just a little bit? My encouragement to you is not to be intimidated. You don't need to be. The Bible is the inspired Word of God, his truth for our lives. God wants his Word to be a blessing to us. And it will be! It just takes time and effort.

The first place to start is not to read a single Bible passage and try to figure out what it means but to read the entire section or chapter or book around that passage. Then find out what other students of the Bible have said using either commentaries or searching online. There's a wealth of collective wisdom and insight by Christians around the world!

It is my prayer that Pastor Mike's messages and the four additional examples we dug into will give you greater confidence in reading the Bible with understanding.

God bless your journey to know him deeper.

# About the Writers

**Pastor Mike Novotny** has served God's people in full-time ministry since 2007 in Madison and, most recently, at The CORE in Appleton, Wisconsin. He also serves as the lead speaker for Time of Grace, where he shares the good news about Jesus through television, print, and online platforms. Mike loves seeing people grasp the depth of God's amazing grace and unstoppable mercy. His wife continues to love him (despite plenty of reasons not to), and his two daughters open his eyes to the love of God for every Christian. When not talking about Jesus or dating his wife/girls, Mike loves playing soccer, running, and reading.

**Dr. Bruce Becker** currently serves as the executive vice president for Time of Grace. He is also a respected and well-known church consultant, presenter, advisor, podcaster, and author. He has served as lead pastor of two congregations; as a member of several boards; and on many commissions, committees, and task forces. In 2012 he completed his professional doctorate in leadership and ministry management. Bruce and his wife, Linda, live in Jackson, Wisconsin.

# About Time of Grace

Time of Grace is an independent, donor-funded ministry that connects people to God's grace—his love, glory, and power—so they realize the temporary things of life don't satisfy. What brings satisfaction is knowing that because Jesus lived, died, and rose for all of us, we have access to the eternal God—right now and forever.

To discover more, please visit timeofgrace.org or call 800.661.3311.

## Help share God's message of grace!

Every gift you give helps Time of Grace reach people around the world with the good news of Jesus. Your generosity and prayer support take the gospel of grace to others through our ministry outreach and help them experience a satisfied life as they see God all around them.

**Give today at timeofgrace.org/give or by calling 800.661.3311.**

Thank you!